SAT
RAY

HEROES & HEROINES

Amitava Nag is an independent film scholar and critic. He has been writing extensively on cinema for the last nineteen years in *The Hindu, The Wire, News18.com, Outlook, CNN-IBN Live, The Statesman, Deep Focus* and *Himal Southasian*, to name a few. He has also been writing and editing the film magazine, *Silhouette*, for seventeen years.

Nag has authored books on cinema, including *Beyond Apu—20 Favourite Film Roles of Soumitra Chatterjee* and *Reading the Silhouette: Collection of Writings on Selected Indian Films.* He also writes poetry and short fiction both in Bengali and English. His first collection of short stories in English and Bengali are *Radha* and *Atma Abamanana Bishayak Ek-Dui Katha*, respectively, apart from a collection of poetry, *Kichhuta Sindur Bakita Golap.*

He lives in Kolkata.

It says a lot about Manik-da's enduring stature as one of the world's leading film-makers that his films continue to be written about to this day. Amitava Nag's is an interesting addition to the corpus, chronicling and analysing some of the significant protagonists who brightened Ray's cinema and the actors who brought them alive onscreen. I have been fortunate to have portrayed five memorable characters in Manik-da's films. I look forward to Amitava's fresh insights on such engaging and diverse array of characters—Indir Thakrun, Apu, Charu, Feluda, Maghanlal Meghraj, Pikoo and more in this book. His perspectives on this aspect of Ray's magnificent legacy will, I am sure, engage and enrich us.

—Sharmila Tagore

Charulata, in Satyajit Ray's film Charulata, *is the most accomplished role that I have ever acted in. It remains an unforgettable film and with it, my role as Charu remains immortal. Satyajit Ray had a very distinct and unique style of handling his actors. He didn't instruct us much, but he was capable of bringing out the best from the actors.*

Casting and acting remain important aspects of his cinema. I don't know if there is any other full-length book in English that focuses on the actors and the different character profiles of Ray's cinema. In this regard, Amitava's book tends to be a unique one. I hope it will help the reader uncover and understand Ray's enigmatic prowess in making most of his actors give brilliant performances. I wish Amitava all the success with this book.

— Madhabi Mukherjee

SATYAJIT RAY'S
HEROES & HEROINES

Amitava Nag

Foreword by Soumitra Chatterjee

RUPA

Published by
Rupa Publications India Pvt. Ltd 2019
7/16, Ansari Road, Daryaganj
New Delhi 110002

Sales Centres:
Allahabad Bengaluru Chennai
Hyderabad Jaipur Kathmandu
Kolkata Mumbai

ISBN: 978-93-5333-344-7

First impression 2019

10 9 8 7 6 5 4 3 2 1

The moral right of the author has been asserted.

Printed at Replika Press Pvt. Ltd, India

CONTENTS

FOREWORD

সৌমিত্র চট্টোপাধ্যায়

ডব্লিউ থ্রি টি সি - নাইন, ফেজ সিক্স
গল্ফ গ্রিন আরবান কমপ্লেক্স
কোলকাতা – ৭০০০৯৫
দূরভাষ: ২৪৭৩ – ৭৮০৪
মোবাইল: ৯৮৩১১ ৫০০৩১

Satyajit Ray is a mentor to me. I have been an avid admirer of this multifaceted genius and how he could amalgamate so many different forms of art within his creation.

Manik-Da had a tremendous eye for details and that is reflected in the different characters that he created on screen, even the apparently insignificant ones.

I am not sure if there has been any book in English that covers the different profiles that he chalked out in his cinema. This book, in that sense, deals with Manik-Da's art from a new perspective.

I am conversant with Amitava's writing and believe that the book will be able to do justice to its goal. I wish Amitava and the book all the success.

Soumitra Chatterjee

28-11-2018

INTRODUCTION

My earliest remembrance of watching a film on Television goes back to the early '80s. It was a Saturday afternoon film for which the entire neighbourhood would wait for the whole week— 'Sanibar-er boi', meaning 'Saturday's film' in Bengali, as it was popularly known. Those were the days of black and white Television with wooden frames and sliding doors in the front. Back then, we didn't have a TV at home. My academician parents thought it to be a major distraction—not to our studies as such but more to our overall 'mental growth'. We were almost never allowed to watch the Saturday Bengali films at our neighbour's house. No wonder, the Sunday afternoon Hindi films were a big 'NO' until we were much older.

Growing up in the '80s without an idea of Hindi cinema had its own pitfalls. When friends swooned over Amitabh Bachchan, Mithun Chakraborty or even Rajesh Khanna, for me, they were just performers in the songs that I would accidentally watch in Television programmes such as *Chitrahaar* or *Rangoli,* while visiting someone's home. For many of my friends and myself, reading and football made up our world.

The first Bengali film that I watched on Television was probably recommended by someone from the neighbourhood—a children's film by the author of the Feluda series. For quite a long time, Satyajit Ray, to many like me, was an author of popular children's stories, including the detective Pradosh C. Mitter (a.k.a. Feluda) and the elderly scientist Professor Shonku, apart from a number of spine-chilling science fiction stories.

Ray was the son of Sukumar Ray and the grandson of Upendrakishore Ray Chowdhury. Upendrakishore's *Chheleder Ramayan* and *Chheleder Mahabharat* were an early initiation into the epics for many Bengali kids, including myself. His other stories based on folklore, and the popular *Goopy Gyne Bagha Byne* (on which Ray made his famous musical film of the same name), are read with the same avid interest even today. Though Sukumar had passed away prematurely in his thirties, he was probably one of the most influential Bengali poets of his time, whose nonsense rhymes were—and still are unparalleled and unrivalled. Upendrakishore started the family magazine, *Sandesh*, in 1913, which Sukumar took over after his father's demise until his own death in the '30s. Eventually, in 1961, Satyajit Ray and the poet Subhas Mukhopadhyay revived it. To sustain *Sandesh*, Ray started writing, and the stories soon became immensely popular. These stories and novels, targeted at teenagers and young adults, hold readers captive even today—and by Ray's own admission, the royalty from his writing sustained his family financially!

There had been quite a few popular characters for

teenagers in Bengali fiction during the '70s and '80s. Bengali literature has been very rich through the ages and that applies to children's literature as well. We never had any dearth of literary heroes back then, and their authors were demigods to us. To me, Satyajit Ray was the creator of my favourite detective, Feluda. I knew Ray was also a film-maker, but as I mentioned earlier, cinema was not a medium we indulged in. My first Saturday afternoon film happened to be *Sonar Kella*, which was one of the Feluda stories I had not read. Watching the colour film in a black and white Television didn't rob it of the magic it first created on an impressionable mind. Feluda on screen matched my imagination to the fullest; then onwards, Soumitra Chatterjee (who played Feluda) became a favourite, which he is even today, along with his mentor Satyajit Ray. However, at that time, I was a bit unsure about the power of Ray as a film-maker. I was under the impression that Ray's task was slightly easy in the film since the character was his own literary creation. Fortunately for me, a few months later, I watched his debut film *Pather Panchali*—the rest, as they say, is history.

I had already read *Pather Panchali* and *Aparajito*—the two volumes written by Bibhutibhusan Bandyopadhyay— and in no time, he had become my favourite Bengali novelist. Apu, the iconic character in the novels, haunted my imagination all the time, and like generations of Bengalis, I often loved to think of myself as Apu. Ray's Apu in *Pather Panchali* was that quintessential Apu of my imagination; if I had created any other image of him while reading the story, I wouldn't remember anymore. The genius of Ray was in making all his characters believable to his audience from his very first film.

Since the magical experience of watching *Pather Panchali*, the film-maker attained an elevated position in my mind. This is extremely important, since I watched the film after three decades of its first release and even then it remained a cinematic experience unique to me. Nothing I had watched before could match up. To a city-bred boy who had, till then, never seen a village, the depiction of rural life was so vivid and believable that it was essentially unreal. Henceforth, in those pre-YouTube, pre-DVD and pre-Torrent days, I would slowly but surely try to watch most of his films, and my admiration of the master knew no bounds. Along with Ritwik Ghatak's deeply passionate and personal film-making style, Ray's eloquent classical charm held me captive since my days of youth.

What appeal do Ray's films have? Without being didactic, one can safely say that Ray's cinema gives Bengalis a space to breathe, the same way as Bengali literature does with its richness. Ray in cinema was almost equivalent to Tagore in literature. He is a prized possession like Tagore—both admired and revered—but the people of the community have seldom internalized their creative philosophies. Like any great form of art, Ray's cinema is simple in its essence and profoundly deep in its eternal appeal and understanding. Thereby, it lets the viewer access it at multiple levels, based on the individual's capacity and mindset. *Goopy Gyne Bagha Byne* is one such example that can be perceived at different planes and at each of them, the experience is gratifying. In most of the cases, Ray has delivered within the rubrics of narrative storytelling. Neither has he experimented much with the cinematic form the way the 'nouvelle vague' directors, the great Russian masters, several European directors and some of the later Indian film-makers have, nor have most of his films deviated from the social strata they depicted. Ray mostly portrayed the educated, Bengali middle-class, whose financial status is not a burden on their emotional and philosophical one. Here, he is markedly different from Mrinal Sen, his contemporary, who had more effectively explored the lower-middle-class segments of society, or Shyam Benegal, who deliberated on the lower rungs of the society. It is this educated Bengali middle-class that has supported and upheld Ray's cinema; he has generally fulfilled the expectation of his audience. At the heart of

Ray's cinema is this wholesome narrative congruity that keeps his audience happy and content. An important aspect of his craft is Ray's brilliant casting and the general acting prowess, which is mostly above-average when compared to mainstream Indian cinema.

In an interview to *Frontline* magazine, Satyajit's blue-eyed boy Soumitra Chatterjee commented, 'Before Ray, there had been good acting in Bengal, but confined to a few gifted persons. Ray's achievement is that he made the whole cast act in the naturalistic mode, the novice and the seasoned buttressing each other. He brought stylistic unity to their cinematic expression.'[1]

Ray (also referred to as Manik-da), who was an ardent admirer of Hollywood movies, observed keenly how the industry moulded stories and design and composed their sets and the frames to suit the talents of big and bankable stars. In Bengal, as well, there were stars during the '30s until the early '50s who were popular, like Pramathesh Barua, Kanan Devi and Chhabi Biswas, apart from stalwart character actors including Ahindra Chaudhuri, Bikas Roy and Pahari Sanyal. Ray had a certain distaste for the traditional method of acting in Bengali cinema in those days, and that was probably one of the primary reasons (the other may be budgetary

---

[1]Soumitra Chatterjee interview, 'The Genius of Satyajit Ray Issue', *Frontline*, 20 December 1991, p. 87.

constraints in taking professional actors) he chose to cast mostly non-actors in *Pather Panchali*. He has written in his book, *Our Films Their Films,*

> The Trilogy was one work of mine which was conceived entirely without reference to available acting material. As a result, most of the parts had to be filled by newcomers. On the other hand I wrote *Paras Pathar* with Tulsi Chakraborty in mind, *Nayak* was written for Uttam Kumar, *Kanchenjungha*, *Devi* and *Jalsaghar* for Chhabi Biswas. Many stories never get beyond the stage of completion because they prove uncastable.[2]

After the first two films, in *Paras Pathar* and *Jalsaghar*, Ray took full time professional actors in Tulsi Chakraborty and Chhabi Biswas, respectively. What is important here is to understand how he changed the pattern of acting—even of veterans—and ensured that there is parity. This is in essence an opposite of the star-concept, where every element of a film moves to portray the star as a larger than life character.

In a rare interview in 1978, Ray had been, uncharacteristically, a bit harsh towards his actors when he said,

---

[2]Satyajit Ray, 'Some Aspects of My Craft', *Our Films Their Films*, Orient Longman Private Limited, 2006, p. 65.

I envy Bergman's stock company. In Bengal, or even for that matter, we don't have professionals of that caliber, no one like Bibi Anderson or a Liv Ullman. They are brilliant virtuoso performers and Bergman can devise parts for them, where they can show the subtlest of emotions and the strongest outbursts of passion. We don't have actors of that calibre. So, stories like *Persona* or *Scenes from a Marriage* are out. My films are more like... I use the analogy with painting...Bonnard, where the human figure has not much more importance than the table, the fruits, the flowers, the landscape, the window, the door... It's all sort of a blend, very close to some Japanese directors.[3]

There is no doubt about the veracity and range of Bergman's actors, and yet none can deny the powerful and authentic rendition of Chhabi Biswas in *Jalsaghar*, Soumitra Chatterjee in *Apur Sansar* and *Charulata*, Madhabi Mukherjee in *Charulata* and Tulsi Chakraborty in *Paras Pathar*. Ray's characters have been real and relatable and his marshalling of his actors ensured that they breathe life into them.

Not only did Ray cast non-actors in the first two

---

[3]Interview with Sasthi Brata, 20 August 1978, excerpted from *IFSON: Special Ray Number*, August 1992, p. 35

films, he had, with impunity, brought in new faces to act out his characters. This is, again, one of the high points of his cinematic craft, wherein he constantly changed the faces of his protagonists (with the exception of Soumitra Chatterjee, who acted in fourteen of Ray's twenty-seven feature films). It seems that it is not because he didn't have Bergman's stock actors, but that he wanted to break any potential monotony. He also did this when the profile of an existing actor didn't match the image of the character that Ray had in his mind. As Soumitra found out when he wanted to play Goopy in *Goopy Gyne Bagha Byne*:

> ...the profile of Goopy was that of a poor village farmer...he had to have a certain raw, rural look which I lacked. I kept on telling Manik-da that if you give me a chance I will do well. I was quite confident of that. He never discouraged anyone so he would smile and then say, 'I know you will do the role very well. But it doesn't match with the image of Goopy that I have in my mind.' I had nothing to say after this. But after I watched the film I told Manik-da that Tapen Chatterjee who played the role did it from within and I probably wouldn't have done justice to the role the way he did.[4]

---

[4]'The Elusive Roles of Ray's Man Friday', *The Hindu*, Mumbai edition, 24 January 2016, http://www.thehindu.com/todays-paper/tp-national/

The same thing happened again with Ray's last film *Agantuk,* as Soumitra recollects, 'Manik-da told me "your image will make the audience believe that this stranger cannot be anything but a nice, honest person. But I want to have some suspense, that's why the person needs to be a little grotesque in his mannerisms", I had nothing more to tell him but accept.'[5] This surety of his profiles actually presented us with a lot of characters which remain etched in Bengali cinema's history, as well as new actors. The three most prominent ones are Soumitra Chatterjee, Sharmila Tagore and Aparna Sen. Soumitra went on to become one of the nation's finest actors and a romantic hero, a star whose bankability was second only to the matinee idol Uttam Kumar, a multifaceted cultural icon, a poet, a writer-director-actor of Bengali theatre, a magazine editor, a painter, an elocutionist and so on. Sharmila Tagore, who debuted with Chatterjee in the third part of *The Apu Trilogy*, *Apur Sansar,* went on to act in the Bombay film industry and became one of the most successful heroines of the '70s, occasionally returning to Calcutta to act in Bengali films, including those by Ray. Aparna Sen, on the other, debuted in *Samapti* (the hero again

---

tp-mumbai/the-elusive-roles-of-rays-man-friday/article8147188.ece, accessed on 15 May 2017.
[5]ibid.

is Soumitra) as a teenage bride, Mrinmoyee, and soon became a successful Bengali heroine before transcending to become one of the most prominent film-makers of India. Not only had Ray launched these three stalwarts, he had also introduced newcomers regularly—Barun Chanda in *Seemabaddha*, Dhritiman Chatterjee in *Pratidwandi* and Pradip Mukherjee in *Jana Aranya,* to name some.

Regarding his handling of actors, Ray had been categorical:

> I do not think it is important to discuss a part thoroughly with an actor, but if he so wishes, I have no fetish against obliging him. Sometimes, with a minimum of guidance, an actor provides me with exactly what I want. Sometimes I have to try an impose a precise manner, using the actor almost as a puppet... Since it is the ultimate effect on the screen that matters, any method that helps to achieve the desired effect is valid.[6]

His actors have generally represented myriad views. Soumitra, for example, always had liberties with Ray, 'Manik-da seldom used to direct me a lot, I could sense what he wanted. Only in *Shakha Proshakha* (1992)

---

[6]Satyajit Ray, 'Some Aspects of My Craft', *Our Films Their Films*, Orient Longman Private Limited, 2006, p. 66.

he would discuss the role in more detail since I was playing a mentally deranged person.'[7] The only Ray film that Om Puri acted in was *Sadgati* (made primarily for TV). Puri was categorical, 'It's all nonsense that he doesn't allow the actors to move. He gives actors a lot of freedom. He is meticulously prepared with his paper work, but he leaves a margin of improvisation.'[8] For Shabana Azmi, who acted in Ray's only Hindi feature film *Shatranj Ke Khilari,* the experience was mixed: 'With Sanjeev (Kumar), I found he was very particular and told him exactly what he wanted. With Saeed and me, he left it to us and gave us the independence to do the scenes the way we liked.'[9]

In the twenty-seven feature films that Ray directed, there are numerous profiles of the middle-class across gender, age and economic conditions. There are characters like Apu, Amal, Charu, as well as the disillusioned ones in Arindam, Siddhartha and Dr Gupta. From 1955 until his last film in 1992,

---

[7]'The elusive roles of Ray's Man Friday', *The Hindu*, Mumbai edition, 24 January 2016, http://www.thehindu.com/todays-paper/tp-national/tp-mumbai/the-elusive-roles-of-rays-man-friday/article8147188.ece, accessed on 15 May 2017.

[8]Om Puri interview to Deepa Gahlot, 'Respectful, but Reserved', *Screen*, 30 March 1992, p. 26.

[9]Shabana Azmi interview to Deepa Gahlot, 'I Admire Him So Much', *Screen*, 20 March 1992, p. 26.

Ray's cinema mirrored and identified the Bengali middle-class. His films are inundated with numerous cameo roles which stick out as memorable performances and are oft referenced and cited in popular culture. While there are several books—serious, academic, or for the common reader—on the art and craft of Ray's cinema, there aren't many (especially in English) which actually deal with his prolific actors and the iconic characters played by them in his cinema. This book sets out to remember these important characters in Ray's films.

In *Satyajit Ray's Heroes and Heroines*, I have followed a two-pronged approach: On one hand, I have discussed the likes of Chhabi Biswas, who represented the patriarchal father figure in three Ray films, Uttam Kumar, who played the 'hero' in *Nayak,* and Soumitra Chatterjee, whose range is too wide to fit him into well cut-out definitions. I have also discussed the 'classical' woman in the roles Madhabi Mukherjee portrayed, or Sharmila Tagore's rendition of the 'modern' woman (apart from her roles in her first two outings in Ray's cinema). On the other, I have charted a profile of the 'city hero', which was played out by four different actors in as many films, or the different characters who were the 'bad' men, if not 'villains' (a term that Ray detested). This book, hence, is a mesh of characters as well as the actors playing the different roles.

The idea for such a book came after I had actually finished my book on Soumitra Chatterjee (*Beyond Apu: 20 Favourite Film Roles of Soumitra Chatterjee*). There has been a dearth of quality material written on Bengali actors in English, and in today's globalized world, where regional identities are getting slowly, but surely, infused, such a compilation is necessary. At a time when there is tremendous value for archival material, I felt the world should know a lot more about these phenomenal actors and their superlative abilities. Being regional actors, it is difficult to discuss them at length individually in separate books. However, I have tried to group some of them under the umbrella of the towering Satyajit Ray. He acted as the vehicle for these actors to go the farthest they could have travelled. This book is a tribute to their magnificent performances. In being so, it is also a personal tribute to Satyajit Ray—from someone who is an inconsequential admirer of his craft and feels fortunate to have grown up reading his books and watching his brand of cinema.

In times when, in the name of homogeneity, sub-standard acting and cinema are being paraded as meaningful, it is probably necessary to step back in time and relish some of Satyajit Ray's masterpieces and marvel at the characters depicted therein. If this book makes readers go back to Ray's films again and savour his art in the light of the discussions contained here, I will consider my work to be a success.

CHHABI BISWAS,
THE ARISTOCRATIC PATRIARCH

In the fourth National Film Awards, in 1956, the award for the Best Film was given to Tapan Sinha's *Kabuliwala*, based on Rabindranath Tagore's immortal tale of the same name. *Kabuliwala* went abroad and won many a laurel for Sinha, as well as for Indian cinema. Amongst others, it won the Silver Bear Extraordinary Prize of the Jury at the Berlin Film Festival in 1957. In his memoir, *Chalachchitra Ajibon*, Tapan Sinha mentions that in the press conference in Berlin that year, 'He (Chhabi Biswas) was asked by the international Press as to which actor in world cinema he would like himself to be compared with. Chhabi-da thundered: "Only the Barrymores". He meant not just one but both the Barrymore brothers combined—Lionel and John. He had that confidence.'[1]

Chhabi Biswas started his acting career in 1936 in Tinkari Chakraborty's *Annapurnar Mandir*, though he truly made a mark in Debaki Bose's *Nartaki* (1940). There was no looking back after that, in a career spanning over twenty-six years before his accidental death in a car crash in 1962 shortly after he played the rich aristocrat Indranath Choudhuri in Satyajit

[1]Tapan Sinha, *Chalachchitra Ajibon*, edited by Shamik Bandyopadhyay, Dey's Publishing, 2009, p. 22. (Translation by the author).

Ray's first colour film *Kanchenjungha*. In these twenty-six years, Biswas acted in well over 250 films, much more than even Uttam Kumar, who ruled the Bengali screen for three decades from the early '50s till 1980. Chhabi Biswas never quite played the romantic hero role. Yet, his popularity was no less than the heroes of the time. In many of the films, he didn't even have substantial screen time, yet, more often than not, left an indelible mark on their narratives. The misfortune of Bengali cinema was in typecasting him as the tyrannical, serious father figure, whose only aim in life is to ensure that the hero and the heroine don't get united. This monochrome shade, along with his experience in theatre, lent a dramatic distinction to his style of acting which may seem overtly theatrical at times. Yet, to Biswas's credit, he had the ability and prowess within him to break from the mould whenever required—be it the three Ray films that he acted in, or in Tapan Sinha's *Kabuliwala*. This manoeuvring of style made him unique and elevated him from the likes of Kamal Mitra, who also revelled in the 'angry' father role.

Kabuliwala, based on a short story by Rabindranath Tagore, was probably the first film that catapulted Biswas's glory to altogether new heights and made his name familiar within the international film circuits. He played an Afghan gypsy staying in Calcutta (erstwhile

Kolkata) who befriends a young Bengali girl, Mini. The uneven chemistry between the two individuals, that transcended age, language, religion, gender and socio-economic status, makes the film so endearing. This is, however, overlooking the fact that in *Kabuliwala*, Chhabi Biswas sported horrendous makeup, which forced a critic from *The Times* to comment, 'He is so good that he makes you forget about his beard'.[2] At the age of fifty-six when he played Rahmat, the Afghan fruit seller in Calcutta, Biswas used his heavy built physique and imposing features to his advantage to produce a riveting performance. In 1961, to mark the birth centenary of Rabindranath Tagore, Hemen Gupta filmed *Kabuliwala* in Hindi under Bimal Roy Productions, casting the legendary Hindi actor Balraj Sahni in the lead role. Balraj Sahni was already a formidable actor, thanks to his exemplary rendition of Sambhu Mahato in *Do Bigha Zameen* (1953, dir: Bimal Roy), which received international recognition. However, in comparison to Biswas's Rahmat, Sahni's characterization lacked the élan that Biswas could bring out so aptly in his portrayal. The power of his acting is such that for generations of filmgoers, Chhabi Biswas as Rahmat remained the epitome of the Kabuliwalas on the streets

---

[2]ibid.

of Calcutta, so much so that they were universally referred to as 'Rahmat'. The flow of Afghan migrants who had come to Calcutta in the early part of the last century to do trade—mostly in dry fruits—has dwindled over the last few decades. Yet, the last representatives of the Kabuliwalas in Calcutta, even today, take pride in being compared to the iconic character. The film became so popular that one can find a Russian version of the Bengali film on YouTube, having the title cards in the same language as well. The simple, humanist appeal of the film can be thought of as a predecessor of the acclaimed Iranian films of the '90s, such as Jafar Panahi's *White Balloon* (1995).

The wide spectrum of Chhabi Biswas's acting can be illustrated through another film from the same year, which was recognized as the best Bengali film of 1956. *Ek Din Ratre* (1956) was a RK Films production, starring Raj Kapoor in his maiden Bengali film. The film was doubly important since it was directed by Sombhu Mitra, the scion of Bengali theatre. Chhabi Biswas played the role of a drunken, happy-go-lucky, unimportant man and excelled in it—a stark contrast from the stoic Rahmat of *Kabuliwala*. The film also had the famous song 'Ei Duniyay Bhai Sob e Hoy', picturized on Biswas prodding along the city at night, and it remains popular even today. Two other off-beat roles for Chhabi Biswas were

Headmaster (1959) and *Dada Thakur* (1962). In *Headmaster*,

Biswas plays the role of a retired Headmaster who comes to the ruthless city of Calcutta with his family of young kids in search of a job after retirement. It is hardship and his clash with the others around him on questions of morality that sets him apart...a very subdued performance yet playing the retired school teacher under the skin, Biswas makes him completely believable. In the end when he is stripped off from his job since he didn't comply, rather he started educating the uneducated staff of the company, it is difficult not to empathize with him. In that he represents the typical Bengali middle-class educated individual who may be poor from an economic standpoint but who definitely has a wealth of moral virtues. This is a characterization in which Soumitra Chatterjee excelled much later in the '80s, but back then even for Biswas as well this was a different profile.[3]

Dada Thakur was filmed in the same year that Biswas acted in *Kanchenjungha*. But a sensible audience cannot but make out the depth of his performances in the two

---

[3]Amitava Nag, 'Chhabi Biswas—Inimitable and Indomitable', *Silhouette*, 12 July 2015, http://learningandcreativity.com/silhouette/chhabi-biswas/, accessed on 15 May 2017.

completely different roles. *Dada Thakur* is:

> ...a bio pic of Bengali maverick writer and social critic Sarat Chandra Pandit. Dada Thakur remains an affable character in the Bengali psyche for his fearless stance against the hypocrisy of the Bengali babus or the high-handedness of the British governance. Contrary to the other haughty characters, as Dada Thakur, Chhabi Biswas played a down-to-earth man who is immensely talented, with a heart of gold—he never misses a smile.[4]

RAY FILMS

In an article written in 1963, Ray emphasized that 'I would cast Chhabi Biswas, our greatest actor, in the leading role of the zamindar whose passion for staging lavish musical entertainments brings about his ruin.'[5] In a later interview in Bengali, in 1970, he elaborated,

> It is not that initially I liked Chhabi babu's acting very much. However, he was quite capable in a particular type of theatrical, professional acting. I felt he may fit into the character of Biswambhar

---

[4]ibid.

[5]Satyajit Ray, 'Winding Route to a Music Room', *Our Films Their Films*, ed, 2006, p. 45.

Roy in *Jalsaghar*. He had that tenor of an aristocratic patriarch. But when we were shooting I found out that there were two things terribly missing in him. Firstly, he didn't know how to ride a horse and secondly he had almost no sense of music. That was a disadvantage. Now I feel those scenes where he was shown enjoying music, his reactions should have been more trained and knowledgeable. But I had taken him two more times after that since I had a very good rapport with him by the time we completed the shooting of *Jalsaghar*. He would let me guide him, which he didn't for any other director. Whenever I have taken him it was in the role of an old-school patriarch—there was no one else in the Bengali film industry who could act in those roles. Whenever there are long dialogues and sustained expressions you need some competent, professional acting which he could deliver with ease.[6]

Andrew Robinson expanded on Biswas's lack of musical sense and commented that Ray,

...did insist, though, that Biswas learn how to fake the playing of an *esraj* so that he could be seen

---

[6]'Prothom Chitranatya, Prothom Peshadar Obhineta', *Nijer Aynay Satyajit*, Bawdweep, 2012, pp 29–30. (Translation by the author).

accompanying his son's singing of the scales. 'He did a very convincing job—I don't know how—through sheer grit, I think.' He also asked Biswas to do something much simpler: to lift one finger of his right hand while he was listening to the strains of dancing coming from Ganguli's house. Biswas had no idea why he was doing this, but in fact, to musical connoisseurs, this makes it clear that Roy knows the rhythmic cycle of the dance music. Later, during the mixing, it gave Ray real satisfaction to coincide the lifting of that finger with the precise beat of the music on the soundtrack.[7]

In *Jalsaghar,* we find an ageing zamindar, Biswambhar Roy, who has to deal with a sagging financial fortune and the ignominy of the rise of a petty moneylender, Ganguli, who has been trying to be his competitor. Chhabi Biswas carried Roy on his shoulders—from the flashbacks when his zamindari was in full swing, to the end when we see him battered and almost ruined. Near the end, he takes up a challenge from Ganguli to host the most promising dancer to perform in his zamindari. It is an expensive affair, and, more so, it means that the music room, which was defunct for a while, will again be lit up to the rhythms of Kathak.

---

[7]Andrew Robinson, *Satyajit Ray: The Inner Eye*, Rupa and Co, 1990, p. 118.

There is a definitive scene where we find Biswambhar Roy entering his music room. He looks as if he is a miniature ape looking up at the drawings of his ancestors, moving from one to the next and finally looking at himself in the mirror. The face wears a forlorn look, vacant, as if he is looking at himself after a long time. Chhabi Biswas, whom even Ray found mostly adept in theatrical exaggerations, looks so vulnerable, as if his domineering veneer has lost its sheath. Like many great creative acting pieces, here as well, Biswas uses minimal techniques to convey the most. He gives a blank look, then softly waves his palm as if to dispel the omen—as if it is that easy to waive off. The inner conflicts of a zamindar rife with pain and helplessness in finding his own aristocracy losing out to the industrial capitalist with a lot of money comes to fore. Ray's full empathy towards the feudal codes of morality and their fragrant cultural patronage is evident in the way the film integrates music within its narrative pace. As Andrew Robinson comments,

> Whether strutting around in sparkling white with a cockade and a riding crop, glancing in private at his meagre 'purse' for the dancer with disdainful resignation, subduing the vulgar Ganguli with a flick of his ivory cane, or staggering in drunken

elation and depression around the music room, he is a formidable presence.[8]

If Biswambhar Roy is one surface of the prism reflecting Chhabi Biswas's extraordinary theatrical abilities, the other one is definitely Indranath Choudhuri of Ray's *Kanchenjungha,* shot six years later. As opposed to the feudal Roy, who despises the newly cropped up capitalist industrial businessmen, in *Kanchenjungha* Biswas played Choudhuri, who is an industrialist and the dictatorial head of a wealthy family. He is immensely influenced by the British rulers and loves being subservient to them. He actually takes a lot of pride in his western manners and habits. Both Biswambhar and Indranath, to an extent, are two sides of the same coin—overbearing, proud and someone who, by virtue of his social status, likes to belittle others. Yet, while there is a lot of empathy towards Biswambhar, Satyajit has little sympathy for Indranath. This remains a latent political statement on Ray's part, chiding a section of spineless Indians who took measures to forget about their own cultural upbringings and moral values. Yet, both Roy and Choudhuri find themselves friendless in the midst of their own lonely miens. The film opens with Indranath ready for the planned rendezvous of his

---

[8]ibid.

family, especially his younger daughter, Manisha, with a potential groom—Banerjee—whom Indranath later calls 'an acquisition'. We find Indranath fiddling with his cigar and meeting different people who help shape his character for us. He first meets a western tourist and discusses, rather amiably, his bad luck at not being able to catch a glimpse of the Kanchenjungha due to the mist; next, he meets Jagadish, his brother-in-law and a bird watcher. Jagadish is following a bird whose call he has heard, and is carrying a book about it. Indranath indignantly tells his brother that his only interest in the bird is whether it can be roasted, as he quite impatiently closes the book in Jagadish's hand. Later, as he is walking along with his wife and an Englishman passes by riding a horse, he quips, 'Thank God that there are some Englishmen left, or else, one would forget how to stay fit in one's old age.' Later, to Ashoke, a young unemployed man, he rejoices, 'I am sixty. Too old to care. Whatever comes out of Independence, is for my children to worry about, and for young men like you. What I say is—I live, I exist...and I have a title—the gift of my ex-rulers—I cherish it, I am proud of it.' There is no doubt that any other Indian actor could not have essayed the role of Indranath Choudhuri with the same authenticity as Biswas did.

The only other Ray film that Chhabi Biswas featured

in was *Devi* (1960), as Kalikinkar Choudhuri. This was completely different from his other roles, as he plays an amiable and gentle father figure of a big family. Kalikinkar is a devotee of Goddess Kali, and one night he dreams that his young daughter-in-law, Doyamoyee, is the Kali-incarnate. Unlike the other roles, in portraying Kalikinkar, Biswas brought in an effective shadow of submission to the Almighty on one hand and reciting long passages from Kalidasa's *Raghuvamsa* on the other, in his argument against the allegations of madness levelled at him by his son Umaprasad. He is affectionate to his son and daughter-in-law, yet fierce in his nurturing of religious practices. It is to be observed that Ray has positioned Doyamoyee as much more than just a victim of the blind superstition of Hindu religious practices. She is rather caught between a feudal father-in-law's idiosyncrasies and her husband's Western ideals, which ultimately don't give the latter enough mental strength to combat his father. In *Devi*, Ray has little sympathy for Kalikinkar's feudal dealings and he is distinctly taking sides with Umaprasad, though keeping him weak to alleviate the film's tragedy to new heights. In this regard, the director's vision is altered from that of *Jalsaghar,* where between tradition (the decadent opulence of Biswambhar Roy) and modernity (the industrial encroachment symbolized by Ganguli as a heartless capitalist) the director's empathy was for the former. Hence, for Chhabi Biswas it was a challenge to interpret the director's opposite stances in the two films, but he came up with yet another excellent performance.

The best actor award at the National film awards, known as the Rajat Kamal Award for the Best Actor, started in 1968 as the Bharat Award for the Best Actor. This was long after Chhabi Biswas's demise in 1962 at the age of sixty-one, and thus he was robbed from potentially bagging it at least once, for any of his three significant roles in Ray's cinema. He was truly an international actor and perhaps the first from India to grab foreign attention. Soumitra Chatterjee, Ray's favourite actor and a living legend, acted alongside Biswas in three films—Tapan Sinha's *Kshudito Pashan* in 1960, Satyajit Ray's *Devi* in 1960 and Ajoy Kar's *Atal Jaler Ahwan* in 1962. Their first interaction happened much earlier, though, on the sets of *Jalsaghar,* when Ray introduced a young Soumitra as his hero in the third part of *Apu Trilogy* to Chhabi Biswas. Soumitra recollects his experiences in acting with the legend,

> On the first day when I heard he had arrived, I went to meet him. We exchanged pleasantries and then I told him, 'Chhabi-da, I have something

to ask of you. I will be acting for the first time in my life with you and you can imagine how tense I am. All I want is that you should guide me whenever I go wrong.' I said this very sincerely and honestly. He kept looking at me to gauge if I was serious or not and then said, 'Look, whatever you do in front of the camera, you have to do confidently. Even if you do something wrong, do it confidently.' That was a great piece of advice on how to approach film acting. I made three films with him—*Kshudita Pashan*, *Devi* and *Atal Jaler Ahwan*. The first one we had very little time together and in the second we had Satyajit Ray in between. But in the last one he guided me a lot. Contrary to the popular belief that Chhabi Biswas used to throw his weight around, at least with me he was always cooperative.[9]

As a tribute to his acting laurels, Soumitra once told me in a personal meeting, 'Like most of Ray's characters, with Chhabi-da as well, can you think of any other actor who could act so effectively in these three roles? Probably not.' We know that Soumitra is not wrong in his assessment of Chhabi Biswas in the films of Satyajit Ray.

---

[9]Amitava Nag, *Beyond Apu: 20 Favourite film roles of Soumitra Chatterjee*, Harper Collins India, 2016, p. 158.

THE CITY HEROES

Cinema, the debatable, suggest deletion or correction, had been technology driven right from its inception. Needless to say, it is undoubtedly a very urban mode of expression. It is no surprise hence that the 'city' has been the backdrop of many ground-breaking films in the rich history of cinema. These range from the neo-realist ones set on Italy's streets after World War II, to the lanes and by-lanes of Paris in the films by the French New Wave directors. In early Indian cinema, one of the boldest portrayals involving the city was in Bimal Roy's *Do Bigha Zameen* in 1953.

Many Bengali films of the '50s, or even part of the '60s, looked at the city of Calcutta, which was, in a sense, tormented after Independence. The '50s was when West Bengal was still trying to come to terms with the Partition of undivided Bengal. The Partition caused an influx of millions of Bengalis from across the border into West Bengal as refugees. Calcutta, the crown of the British Empire, suddenly found it inadequate to balance this rise in population. Several leading theatre activists and film-makers, including Ritwik Kumar Ghatak, addressed the Partition and the natural human calamity that it brought in, through their work.

Satyajit Ray was always subtle, and at times, a bit passive in his criticism of the State or the social and human condition, that was largely man-made. His famed compatriots in Ritwik Ghatak and Mrinal Sen were more vocal, more direct and always scathing in their aggression. Ray's style of film-making, which was more classical, held the lens at an objective distance which was neither direct nor aloof. The city did feature in his early films, albeit in a non-intrusive way. In *Apur Sansar,* for example, we find Apu in the midst of the hustle and bustle of Calcutta. However, it is the individual rather than the city which is in focus. Apu's interaction with the city is minimal and almost non-communicative, as if the city is used as a background—static and decidedly indifferent. Even in *Paras Pathar,* where the protagonist's change of fortune is more of an urban fable, we find the presence of the city more as a spectator rather than as an actor.

Ray's first direct tryst with the city was in his masterpiece *Mahanagar (The Big City)* in 1963. Set in the '50s, it deals with the changing social dynamics in the face of an economic crisis. We find the neat Bengali household of Subrata (Anil Chatterjee) and Arati (Madhabi Mukherjee), along with their young son, Pintu, the teenage sister of Subrata named Bani, and Subrata's parents. The parents have come over from their village to stay in the city—an influx that has destabilized the household and hold up a reflection of the city at large. In dire need, Arati has to go out, against familial opposition, to earn a livelihood for the family. Subrata, who has been ambivalent in his stance about his wife's going out for work, soon finds himself incapacitated after losing his job. In one of the opening scenes, Subrata's father laments: 'Oh, Calcutta has changed so radically.' Here he is referring to the general indifference of the citizens, which he finds unacceptable. There are multiple shots on the streets placing Arati and Subrata within the crowd, but not as unique figures (like Apu) dissociated from the melee.

Anil Chatterjee, who played Subrata, appeared in three Ray films before playing the hero in *Mahanagar*. His first role was as a friend of Umaprasad, the hero in *Devi* (1960). It was a small role but an important one, instrumental in defining the changes in Umaprasad. Chatterjee again had a brief appearance as the errant son of the Raybahadur in *Kanchenjungha* (1962). However, his first notable performance in a Ray film was as the postmaster in the first segment (titled *Postmaster*) of the triad *Teen Kanya* (*Three Daughters*) in 1961. Commemorating the birth centenary of Rabindranath Tagore, Ray's *Teen Kanya* was a tribute to the Nobel laureate. Chatterjee reminisced about an incident during the shooting of *Postmaster*:

There was a scene where observing that her clothes were dirty, the postmaster would ask Ratan (the young house-maid working in the postmaster's quarter) if her mother doesn't wash her clothes. The instructions were that she would be silent and when I would ask her again she would tell me that her mother had passed away. During the shooting, even after my second question, she didn't say a thing. I was convinced that Chandana, who played Ratan, had forgotten the dialogue. My facial expression slackened with this realization when suddenly Chandana uttered her dialogue—'Mother is no more'. It was so poignant, but my expression wasn't there as a reaction shot since I had already been distracted moments before. Though I didn't say a thing Manik-da could make out that I was not happy with my performance. He went to Chandana and then bent his towering figure and whispered to her—'You have done a brilliant job. But your Anil uncle has made a small mistake; we will take this shot again, ok?'...any lesser director would have kept Chandana's brilliant expression there, ignoring the fact that the postmaster's reciprocation was equally important.[1]

---

[1]Anil Chatterjee, 'Chitranatya E Onek-khani Obhinoy Kore Rakhe', *Desh* Magazine, 'Special Satyajit Issue', 28 March 1992, pp. 88–89

In his next film with Ray, *Kanchenjungha*, Chatterjee played a character in his twenties, almost ten years younger than his real age. He had his doubts,

> ...but those who act in Satyajit Ray's films are seldom inflicted with any doubt. The director himself triggers a confidence in them. What is this psychological process? Satyajit Ray treats his actors as his friends, he creates an intimate relation where the actor is never aware of the tough task the director has bestowed on him. He creates an atmosphere which is both personal and friendly.[2]

Chatterjee reminisced about a particularly memorable experience during the shooting of the film:

> The bird-watcher character, who is the uncle of Manisha, was carrying an English book on birds. Manik-da was describing the scene to Pahari Sanyal, who was playing the character, when an old man kept coming up to Manik-da and asking him a lot about the bird the character was planning to watch. Manik-da initially wanted to dismiss the enthusiasm of the old man by casually referring to the bird as a 'Himalayan bird'. But this didn't

---

(Translation by author).
[2]ibid., p. 91.

pacify the old man and in the process the shooting got delayed. Manik-da then came up to me and requested me to manage the situation so that the shot could be taken. I went up to the old man and to my utter surprise, found out that he was the famous ornithologist Salim Ali, and it was a book written by him that Pahari-da was actually carrying along with him in the scene.[3]

In multiple interviews, Anil Chatterjee mentioned the freedom Ray gave his actors. Like many others, including Soumitra Chatterjee whose improvisations were more often than not incorporated by Ray, Anil Chatterjee also had the privilege of bringing his sensibilities to make the characters more human. He explains one such instance while filming *Mahanagar*, his last and most memorable appearance in a Ray classic:

There was this scene where Arati was going out to work for the first time and the son was crying. The entire sequence was planned to be shot at one go, the camera was static and so was my position. The shot was not supposed to give me any preference. Just before the shot was to be taken I somehow felt that I needed to do some thing there, so I

---

[3]ibid., pp. 91–92.

asked Manik-da if I could use a matchstick to prick my teeth since the previous shot showed that I had had my lunch. He readily agreed. He was so methodical in his approach, yet he would allow these small things which make the characters more natural and also ease the actors playing the same.[4]

Chatterjee, who acted in films by the greatest directors of his time, was a popular star along with the likes of Uttam Kumar and Soumitra Chatterjee. He moved on to character acting and had many memorable roles to his credit. One of those rare actors who played the central character in multiple films of both Satyajit Ray and his ace compatriot, the maverick Ritwik Ghatak, Chatterjee. He recalls the difference between the two masters:

Ritwik Ghatak was situated at a complete opposite position to Ray in terms of philosophy, attitude and vision. I came to work with Ray after I worked in Ghatak's films. On his way to the shooting spot Ritwik-da was mesmerized by the dance of the Oraon tribe. He later added it in his film. Both of them have made memorable films, but one relishes working within strict discipline whereas the other derives his pleasure from breaking it.[5]

---

[4]ibid., p. 92.
[5]ibid., p. 94.

Though *Mahanagar* was the first Ray film where the city of Calcutta is essentially the central character along with the lead pair, Ray soon after drifted to the more classically romantic genres in films like *Charulata, Goopy Gyne Bagha Byne* or even *Nayak*. In 1969, Ray made *Aranyer Din Ratri,* about four youths who leave the city in search of a break from their mundane lives and settle in the forest of Palamu, in Bihar (now a part of Jharkhand). The film is without doubt one of the finest of Ray's in terms of craftsmanship and in its meditations on human relationships. Thoroughly western in its timbre, the film was well appreciated in the West, but was criticized at home for being aloof at a time when the country, especially Bengal, was up in flames due to the students' armed revolution popularly known as the Naxalite movement. Ray didn't succumb to the charges, but made two films back to back in a span of two years to silence his critics. *Pratidwandi* (1970) and *Seemabaddha* (1971) held the city as a palette from where the director painted his canvas according to his wish. After a gap of two other films, he returned to the subject of the city in *Jana Aranya* (1975) to complete what is known as *The Calcutta Trilogy.* Quite interestingly, Mrinal Sen, the other internationally acclaimed Indian film-maker sharing the same time-span as Ray, made his more political and overtly polemical *Calcutta Trilogy* almost simultaneously—

Interview (1971), *Calcutta 71* (1971) and *Padatik* (1973).

Ray had almost always been clinical in his casting. He ensured that he got the right face and the right characteristics in a person for his central characters. The city heroes of the '70s in all the three films are angst-ridden, robbed of their innocence. They are the other side of Apu, the iconic Ray dreamer played to perfection by Soumitra Chatterjee. Apu's personal losses couldn't rob the gleam in his eyes or his tremendous zeal and goodliness. In the '70s, with the social and economic shifts that the country, in general, and the city of Calcutta, in particular, were going through, that radiant innocent charm was difficult to hold on to. No wonder Ray's heroes of the '70s were disenchanted and confused. To play these roles, Ray chose three different actors to represent the face of youth in the three films— Dhritiman Chatterjee in *Pratidwandi*, Barun Chanda in *Seemabaddha* and Pradip Mukherjee in *Jana Aranya*.

Dhritiman Chatterjee was a Delhi University student when his interest in the medium germinated, largely by watching classics and subsequently in the process of setting up a film society in the University. He recalls,

> I entered cinema just before I entered HTA (advertising agency Hindustan Thompson Associates, later called J Walter Thompson).

I always had an active interest in cinema, and it was reaching a great peak then. I'm talking about the 1960s here. I would devour films, largely Indian and French. Some friends formed one of India's first true film societies, to fan our own enthusiasm. In this exciting process, we contacted people like (Satyajit) Ray and Mrinal-da (Sen). Establishing this contact was, in itself, a huge thrill... While he was casting for *Pratidwandi*, a close friend of mine threw us together. Without any warning, he decided to cast me!... It was exciting... to me, most of the excitement was not in being in front of the camera, but in the joy of watching Ray work. From extremely close quarters! It was great... *Pratidwandi* marked a style change for him—a lot of handheld camera, and shooting in the streets.[6]

Siddhartha of *Pratidwandi* is unemployed. His younger sister works in a company as a secretary to a suave manager—which Siddhartha doesn't like for obvious reasons, apart from the fact that he himself is incapable of earning anything for the family. The youngest brother is a revolutionary and Siddhartha distances himself from him as well. For the first time in a Ray film, we come to see a nurse who doubles as a part-time prostitute. Gulabi in *Abhijan* was Seth Sukhanram's 'kept' woman but the audience was sympathic towards her. However, the nurse in *Pratidwandi* is meant to denote the decadence of virtue and the tattered innocence of the city, which is no longer a citadel of hope but of loss, despair and agony.

Dhritiman's Siddhartha echoed the pathos of the time in his stoic facial expression: 'You would hardly see my character smile. Mine was the role of an angry young man. Fortunately, I got to play a role that I could identify with—a youth in the '70s. While playing my part, I could make out that Ray effortlessly eked out the anti-hero from inside me.'[7] He continues, 'My experience with every director is valuable to me. But Satyajit Ray was a complete film-maker with full control on all aspects of cinema whether it was the screenplay, costumes or cinematography. The most distinguishing characteristic of Satyajit Ray was that he was extremely planned. Before the shoot of a film would begin, he would have worked out all the details.'[8] Chatterjee

---

[7]'Five Of Satyajit Ray's Prominent Heroes Share Their Secrets In an Adda Session', *The Times Of India*, Kolkata, 10 Jan 2012, http://epaper.timesofindia.com/Repository/ml.asp?Ref=VE9JS00vMjAxMi8wMS8xMCNBcjAwMzAw, accessed on 15 May 2017

[8]'Satyajit Ray Was a Complete Filmmaker', *NDTV Movies*, 01 May 2013

would return to Ray's films much later in the master's last two films—*Ganashatru* (1990) and *Agantuk* (1992).

In *Ganashatru*, which was Ray's version of Henrik Ibsen's *An Enemy of the People*, it was a difficult role for Chatterjee, playing a negative character for the first time. He did it marvelously. Chatterjee did feature in films of other directors occasionally when the roles offered suited his tastes. For instance, he acted in a number of Mrinal Sen's films as well, including *Padatik* and *Akaler Sandhane*. Referring to the different styles of Ray and Sen, Dhritiman commented, 'Ray wrote for the actor and so you got into the rhythm very quickly. He had two distinct methods for dealing with actors—either he guided them every step of the way, or gave complete freedom as he did with me.'[9] With Sen, who was more into improvising impromptu, the method was to have the whole crew available during the entire tenure. As Chatterjee observes, '…Mrinal-da was never sure when and what scene he'd be shooting next. He improvised all the time. In *Padatik* for example, no one knew how the film was going to end, least of all himself! I enjoyed

---

http://movies.ndtv.com/regional/satyajit-ray-was-a-complete-filmmaker-says-dhritiman-chatterjee-611800, accessed on 15 May 2017
[9]'Chennai's Bengali Son-in-Law', *The Hindu*, 07 August 2000, http://www.thehindu.com/2000/08/07/stories/13070783.htm, accessed on 15 May 2017.

being a part of that process.'[10]

The second film of *The Calcutta Trilogy* was *Seemabaddha*, which had Ray-veteran Sharmila Tagore play an important character. For the hero, Ray introduced Barun Chanda who was, like Dhritiman, working at an advertising agency. Chanda was working in Clarion and his corporate identity suited him to the role of Shymalendu. However, even before the casting of the film, he had met Ray on the pretext of interviewing him for a journal. Unlike most other Ray heroes, Shyamalendu is a confident young man whose level of self-doubt is visibly low. He is successful at an early stage in his career, which gives him the necessary arrogant swagger about himself. Asim of *Aranyer Din Ratri* (played by Soumitra Chatterjee) is similar to Shyamalendu in this aspect. Both are, to an extent, grounded by the female characters played by Sharmila Tagore in both the films—as Aparna, in *Aranyer Din Ratri,* towards whom Asim gets attracted, and as Tutul, in *Seemabaddha,* who is the attractive sister-in-law of Shyamalendu. The relationship between Tutul and Shyamalendu is not romantic—rather, Tutul acts as a conscience and a sentinel against whom Shyamalendu judges his decadent moral values in his journey to corporate success.

---

[10]ibid.

Chanda's sophistication in his mannerisms and his voice helped him to portray Shyamalendu with ease—the westernized, urban sophistication which was matched only by Uttam Kumar as the superstar in *Nayak*. Chanda never would act again in a Ray film, though he returned to cinema and Television much later. His admiration for Ray, like others, is insurmountable:

> Satyajit was an introvert man and would talk less, which made people think that he was proud and self-centred. But he was not. If someone told him a good joke, he would burst out into laughter. I had even seen tears coming out of his eyes as a result of uncontrollable episodes of laughter… He was quite an organised director and would make films in a pre-planned manner. He would do all the inspection himself. From set design to purchasing costumes, Satyajit was behind everything.[11]

The last film of the trilogy was *Jana Aranya* in 1975. Somnath, the hero—played by another newcomer, Pradip Mukherjee—was similar to Siddhartha in that he was an unemployed youth as well. The film starts with how, during the '70s, the vulnerable education system,

---

[11]'Barun Shares His Experiences with Satyajit Ray', *NewAge*, 9 Feb 2016, http://newagebd.net/200900/barun-shares-his-experiences-with-satyajit-ray/, accessed on 15 May 2017.

with no standardized process, controls the future of the youth in a country where academic results are considered to be the only proof of one's abilities. Somnath becomes a middleman in the business domain of import and export and soon a new world of corruption, vices and dishonesty opens up before him. The realizations and experiences of Siddhartha were limited and passive, whereas for Somnath they are even more stark, brutally dominant and nagging. Pradip Mukherjee had it in his face—an innocent ebullience unlike the somber Siddhartha, and that is why the contrast between his sleazy experiences and his frugal self becomes cinematically telling and pertinent. However, Pradip Mukherjee's entry into Ray's art wasn't smooth. Like many actors with a dream of working in Ray's films, Mukherjee had to wait for quite some time as well:

> I had the dream of becoming a hero in cinema for a long time before I joined films. I had visited Mr Ray a few times then and every time he would say 'Keep in touch, I don't have any work for you now.' I was never disheartened since somehow I had this belief that one day I will definitely get a call from him. Then after sometime I went to his place. I still remember the date. It was 21st December 1974. He told me that he had actually

been looking for me for a while but couldn't reach me. He then called for me again the next day and we talked about cinema for nearly an hour. I later understood, within that easy-flowing discussion he was actually evaluating me. He called me again on 25th December in the afternoon. There were a lot of people at his place. He took me aside and said, 'Read *Jana Aranya,* the novel. I want to cast you as Somnath, the hero.' I can't describe my feelings when I was returning from his place. It seemed that the city had suddenly become colourful.[12]

Mukherjee explains his experience with Ray:

From the Screen test till the last day of shooting, Manik-da would teach me the basics of cinema-acting and the importance of economy of expression. I still treasure the script-reading session, every detail of his film was in his red bound book and the rest was in his brain. I felt the entire film was packed up in his brain in a reel, and while filming, he just transferred the same on to celluloid.[13]

---

[12]'Pradip Mukherjee Interview', *Desh* magazine 'Special Satyajit Issue', 28 March 1992, pp. 131–32 (Translation by author).
[13]ibid., p. 132.

Ray was a master at handling new actors, considering the plethora of them making their debut in his cinema. Mukherjee explains why Ray's handling almost always created magic on screen:

I have acted in the films of a few other directors after *Jana Aranya*. I have seen how most of them fail while handling new actors. I feel selection is not everything. One needs to know how to deal with untapped talents as well, which Manik-da was adept in. He would give a lot of flexibility to his actors but guided them whenever required. I recollect one incident. The scene was that of a phone call from Tapati (played by Aparna Sen) who was my on-screen girl-friend. I had to cut the call after a short conversation. I was not able to do it properly and Manik-da told me—'Do it more romantically.' I was still not able to provide the necessary reaction. He then called me aside and told me, 'You are such a fan of Pramathesh Barua—can't you replace the receiver in a more romantic way? Don't do this scene so mechanically. Keep in mind that the call is from your girl-friend. So you will hesitate about putting down the receiver before she does. Bring that mild confusion, the short wait and

the hesitation before putting down the receiver.'
Needless to say, I could grasp the inner essence of
the scene and do it properly then.[14]

Ray never dealt with the urban city as a character in
any of his subsequent films. His attention, like before,
shifted to individuals and their relationships, along
with period settings as in *Shatranj Ke Khilari* or *Ghare Baire*.
However, the *Calcutta Trilogy* remains probably his last set
of films to be acclaimed internationally as well. It is
also the last time Ray introduced non-actors to play the
central characters. The city heroes of the trilogy remain
as urban profiles who, even today, mirror our existence
and frailties, our moments of transcendence, depths of
bleakness and utter failure.

---

[14]'Pradip Mukherjee Interview', 'Tollygunje O Satyajit', *Saptahik Bartaman*
magazine, 11 April 1992, p. 15 (translation by author).

HUMOUR, THE WAY OF LIFE

Charles Spencer Chaplin once opined, 'Humour is a gentle and benevolent custodian of the mind which prevents us from being overwhelmed by the apparent seriousness of life.' Chaplin's cinema, in its entire gamut of human emotions, has steadfastly depicted the seriousness of life within its most tranquil and sublime humourous structure. As Ray observed in his 1964 article on Chaplin's 1925 masterpiece *The Gold Rush*: 'Watching him, you realize that he must be one of the very few artists of the twentieth century who is able to completely disarm a critic at one moment and, at the next, challenge his sharpest faculties and come out unscathed.'[1] In Indian mainstream cinema in general, and Bengali cinema in particular, humour in its most nuanced form is hard to find. They mostly have comic elements, slapstick to be precise, where the physical acting of comedians provides laugh-breaks in a story of apparent seriousness. In Ray's own oeuvre, one may observe that there is a certain undercurrent of humour which, in most cases, is sublimely wry and more often than not unobservable as comedy. Take, for example, the section in *Samapti* where Amulya goes to meet Mrinmoyee and her parents for the first time as part

---

[1] Satyajit Ray, 'The Gold Rush', *Our Films Their Films*, Orient Longman Private Limited, 2006, p. 168.

of the bride-watching custom. The scene is rife with undiluted humour. It has laugh-worthy moments but is definitely not mindless, trash comedy. Ray's penchant for this lightness appears in most of his other films. Another example may be from *Nayak,* where the hero Arindam meets an old critic on the train who bashes films and the drinking associated with filmstars in equal measure. Apart from this undercurrent of humour in most of his works, Ray has occasionally dealt with comedies and helped them transcend beyond being mere ensembles of comic acts by established comedians. However, he did rely on professional comedians because of their natural finesse—and also probably because of their acceptability to the masses. Yet, in all such cases, the characters went far beyond their comic presence, as full-bodied individuals with frailties and moments of sadness.

RABI GHOSH

Amongst all the comedians of Bengali cinema who have acted in Ray's films, Rabi Ghosh appeared in seven. He was next only to Santosh Dutta, who acted in eight; though it can be argued that barring the last film, Ghosh had more important roles to enact than Dutta. The films in which Ghosh appeared are *Abhijan*

(1962), *Kapurush-O-Mahapurush* (1965), *Goopy Gyne Bagha Byne* (1968), *Aranyer Din Ratri* (1969), *Jana Aranya* (1975), *Hirak Rajar Deshe* (1980) and *Agantuk* (1992). Rabi Ghosh started his career on stage in Utpal Dutt's Little Theatre Group (LTG). His first interaction with Ray happened, coincidentally, when Ray came to watch their play *Angaar* in 1960 (it was a big success at the time). It was in 1961, when Ghosh was acting in Tapan Sinha's sensitive film *Hanshuli Banker Upakatha,* that his first proper meeting with Ray happened:

> I had liked the new type of work in a new media. When one day when I was returning home, I met Bhanu Ghosh on a bus. Bhanu was the Assistant Production Manager of Manik-da's films at that time and was my classmate from school. Bhanu told me that Manik-da was looking for me. Hearing this, I went to Manik-da's then residence at Lake Temple Road that same evening with Bhanu. That was when I first spoke to him directly, and yet I felt as if we had known each other for a long time. Manik-da told me, 'You have to do a role, that of a motor car cleaner.' I can't express my feelings after hearing that.[2]

---

[2]'Rabi Ghosh Interview', *Desh* magazine 'Special Satyajit Issue', 28 March 1992, pp. 130–31 (translation is by author).

Rabi Ghosh played Rama, the sidekick to Soumitra Chatterjee's masterful Narsingh in *Abhijan*—a character which he played with immense sincerity and intimate detail. Though Ray was generally very structured and methodical in his shot taking, yet he did give certain licenses to actors who could improvise well and render appropriately. Recalls Ghosh,

> There was this scene in *Abhijan* where I was supposed to walk away after speaking to Gulabi (Waheeda Rahman). It was a simple scene. Suddenly I realized that there was a buffalo sitting on my way. I just improvised there and jumped over the buffalo, that immediately stood up as I crossed him. I thought Manik-da would not approve and was tense till I heard Manik-da shout at me, 'Fine'. That relieved me.[3]

Ghosh could imbibe in him the style of subdued expression prevalent in most of the acting in Ray's films. There had been exemplary comic histrionics earlier by the inimitable Tulsi Chakraborty in *Paras Pathar* (1958), but Rabi Ghosh ensured he did not follow similar lines. Instead he carved a niche for himself, as Andrew Robinson comments—

---

[3]Ibid.

Rabi Ghosh's funny performance—his first for Ray—had much to do with *Abhijan*'s success and is the best in the film. He based it on days of careful observation of taxi-cleaners at a taxi stand near his home in Calcutta: he imitated their mannerisms and their ways of talking, which often leaves words indistinct. Ray was delighted.[4]

Ghosh's next engagement with Ray was in the comic satire *Mahapurush,* of the two-part film *Kapurush-o-Mahapurush.* Interestingly, here again he plays a sidekick—that of a dishonest god-man (played eloquently by Charuprakash Ghosh). Based on a scathing remark in the form of a short story named *Birinchibaba* by eminent writer Parashuram, Ray unfolds his disbelief in the blind faith borne by individuals (of all classes) in religious practices and the executioners of the same. Unlike the other prevalent comedians of the Bengali screen, including Tulsi Chakraborty, Bhanu Bandyopadhyay, Jahar Roy and Santosh Dutta, Ghosh had a smaller body frame, which he used effectively whenever pitted as a sidekick to heroes having distinctly bigger physiques. In *Aranyer Din Ratri,* he used this feature to build the character of Sekhar. Amidst his three friends, who were better in stature—

[4]Andrew Robinson, *Satyajit Ray: The Inner Eye*, Rupa and Co, 1990, p. 147.

physically and socio-economically—Rabi plays a role resembling a clown, who entertains not only his male friends but also the two women the group befriends during their stay in the jungle. Ghosh's acting, which is different from Tulsi Chakraborty's, is primarily based on an impeccable sense of timing and usage of 'pause' moments in the dialogues. Like any great actor, Ghosh added effective expression through his glances—squinting his eyes and opening them wide—which has remained a hallmark of his style.

The most enduring role of Rabi Ghosh, however, will forever be as Bagha in the legendary film *Goopy Gyne Bagha Byne* and its polemical sequel *Hirak Rajar Deshe*. Based on Ray's grandfather's story for young children, *Goopy Gyne Bagha Byne* depicts two village buffoons—Goopy (a new find in Ray's films—Tapen Chatterjee, an actor with rare skills) and Bagha (Rabi Ghosh)—and their fairytale adventure as they stop a war between two neighbouring kingdoms ruled by estranged brothers. The film remains Ray's top grosser till date. It is lyrical and entertaining with a subtle, simple yet powerful political message to deliver. The sequel, which happens to be more political in nature and written by Ray himself, finds Ghosh and Tapen slip back into their respective roles without a trace of the gap of twelve years. They featured again in the third part of the trilogy, *Goopy Bagha Phire Elo* (1992), written by Ray but directed by his son, Sandip Ray.

In *Jana Aranya*, Ghosh plays Natabar Mitra, a supplier of demands that range from inanimate objects to prostitutes. A dark satire, Ghosh plays the role to perfection with immense comic timing, although the role is devoid of any comic situations. In multiple interviews, Ghosh has mentioned that this is his most favourite role, possibly because he was fed up with his constant identification as a comedy actor. In Ray's last film, *Agantuk*, Rabi Ghosh almost plays himself, as a comedian of Bengali cinema and theatre who accepts that there isn't any scope of doing high-class satire or dark comedy. The role is not as significant as his other illustrious characterizations, which have put him in an international league. Throughout his life, Rabi Ghosh remained indebted to Utpal Dutta for being his mentor in theatre and to Satyajit Ray for his cinema:

> Manik-da never strains his actors. This is my experience from *Abhijan* till *Agantuk*. I feel there is no actor in India who is of the same caliber as him. When he enacts the character to the actors, the philosophy and intellect of the characters come across vividly—we, the actors, can reproduce probably 50-60% of what he shows us through his

acting. He had always allowed me to improvise, maybe because I seldom go overboard. But he does so till he thinks his frame is not disturbed in any way by my improvisation.[5]

SANTOSH DUTTA

Another actor from Ray's comic cinema, whose role could be as iconic as Bagha from the Goopy-Bagha films and live for decades with the same freshness, is Santosh Dutta who played Jatayu in the two Feluda films. Jatayu is an adventure-thriller writer for young adults and almost a comic foil to Feluda, the detective. Written by Ray, the Feluda stories are bestsellers even today. Ray made *Sonar Kella*, the first Feluda film, in 1974 and followed it up with *Joy Baba Felunath* in 1979. Feluda was played by none other than Soumitra Chatterjee, who was Ray's favourite and seemed quite an obvious choice, given the fact that Ray's own illustrations of the character in the novels had an uncanny resemblance to Soumitra. For Jatayu, however, the illustrations in the first few stories were all different before Ray finalized the one that resembled Santosh Dutta after *Sonar Kella* became a big hit. A criminal

[5]Rabi Ghosh Interview, 'Special Satyajit Issue', *Desh* Magazine, 28 March 1992, p. 131 (Translation of Interview Is by Author).

lawyer by profession, Dutta balanced his career with his acting, which flourished late with the Feluda films and gave him his due recognition. Sandip Ray said,

> Baba was extremely fond of Santosh Dutta and always admired him. He had acted in *Parash Pathar* and *Goopy Gyne Bagha Byne*. So, while making Feluda, Santosh Dutta was cast first—even before Baba had zeroed in on Feluda. The earlier drawings of Jatayu didn't resemble Santosh Dutta at all. But his performance in *Sonar Kella* cast such a spell on the audience that Baba decided to draw Jatayu in his likeness.[6]

The two Feluda films ingrained the image of Jatayu deeply into the Bengali psyche. Ray decided that he would not do any more Feluda films after Dutta's untimely demise in 1988. Later, when Sandip Ray started making a series of Feluda films and telefilms, he cast Rabi Ghosh and Anup Kumar to play Jatayu in them. Sandip also tried Bibhu Bhattacharjee, but none of the three could match up to Dutta's legendary personification of Jatayu.

Santosh Dutta, however, featured in a few small

---

[6]'Jatayu Revisited', *Times of India*, 15 Oct 2011, http://timesofindia. indiatimes.com/others/news-interviews/Jatayu-revisited/ articleshow/10364419.cms, accessed on 15 May 2017.

roles in early Ray's films—as program announcer Atanu in *Paras Pathar*, father of a potential bride in *Teen Kanya*, Professor Nani in *Kapurush-o-Mahapurush* and later, as a supplier of raw materials in *Jana Aranya*. His first breakthrough role was in *Goopy Gyne Bagha Byne*, where he portrayed the double roles of the Kings of the two neighbouring states—Shundi and Halla. The King of Shundi is a benevolent one who loves music. He appoints Goopy and Bagha as court musicians. The Halla King is the lost brother of the King of Shundi. An evil prime minister and his accomplice, the magician, poison the Halla King. The magic potion that poisons his mind makes him declare a war against his brother. Santosh Dutta plays both characters with rare astuteness—natural and polite as the Shundi king, and as the Halla-king, his emotions traversing from being child-like—almost an infant—to occasional reactions of rare guile under the effect of the potion. In *Hirak Rajar Deshe*, Dutta plays a scientist who devises 'Jantarmantar'—a machine that brainwashes people.

Feluda was adapted for national Television in Hindi for the short *Kissa Kathmandu Ka* as part of the Television series *Satyajit Ray Presents*, where Sashi Kapoor played Feluda and Mohan Agashe, Jatayu. The nation's audience liked the series to an extent, but it was a disaster for the Bengali audience, who neither accepted

Sashi Kapoor in place of Soumitra Chatterjee, nor agreed with Mohan Agashe's antics as Jatayu.

TULSI CHAKRABORTY

Tulsi Chakraborty was a legendary Bengali actor whose acting prowess had always emerged in sparks and pieces, until he was cast in the central role of Ray's comic masterpiece *Paras Pathar* (1958). Ray shot *Paras Pathar* while he was on a break from filming *Jalsaghar* since the lead actor for the latter, Chhabi Biswas, was occupied with a festival in Berlin. *Paras Pathar* turned out to be one of Ray's masterpieces; his first foray into comedy and much more than a stop-gap film. It was a dream come true for Tulsi Chakraborty, who till then was used sparingly by directors with the prime motive of making the audience laugh.

Chakraborty started his film career in the early '30s, but his first memorable role was in the hilarious comedy film *Saare Chuattor* in 1953. It had an array of comedians, including Bhanu Bandyopadhyay and Jahar Roy, yet Tulsi Chakraborty, as the owner of a mess building (along with Molina Devi, who played his wife), held the focus of the film. *Saare Chuattor* is historically important as well, since it launched the Uttam Kumar–Suchitra Sen pair for the first time in Bengali cinema. They went on to become the most sought-after and discussed pair in films. Ironically, for Tulsi Chakraborty, things didn't change much even after the tremendous success of *Saare Chuattor*.

Tulsi Chakraborty spent his early life like a bohemian. He got himself into a number of occupations, including being a clown in Bose's Circus Party, with whom he went to Burma (now Myanmar). This was where he learnt to speak Urdu and Farsi while communicating with the different inmates of the circus and later became proficient in singing khayals and thumris as well. When he returned to Calcutta, he joined theatre and then moved onto acting in films. In spite of making worthwhile contributions on screen, his remuneration was often very little. Bibhu Bhattacharya, who was a child artist in the early '50s and later played Jatayu in Sandip Ray's five Feluda films, happened to watch Tulsi Chakraborty from close quarters. Bibhu laments the disparity in the treatment of an actor of Chakraborty's merit:

> During those days, the production controllers tried to exploit actors a lot. When we began working, we were given our remuneration as soon as we finished work. I used to get Rs.75 per day... My brother would sign the voucher and, then,

accept my remuneration. One day, Tulsi-da asked my brother how much I get. After hearing my remuneration, he said he would get only Rs.15 per day. I still shudder to think what kind of a disparity that was![7]

This paltry remuneration made Tulsi Chakraborty face immense hardship. Even after his death, his widowed wife was subjected to abject poverty and humiliation. Recalls Bibhu,

Once he was shooting at the East India Studio and he came up to me and asked if I would get a car or not. The reason for this was that he wouldn't get a car to return home and if I got one, he would hitch a ride from me. He would wait till hours on end for me to finish. From lunch till my pack-up time in the evening, he'd sleep on the bench for me to finish work so that he could get a lift ... Actually, he was paid so less that he wanted to save whatever money he could. He would usually take a tram from Tollygunge to Dharmatala. He travelled second class. That took one anna. Then, he would

---

[7]'Tulsi Chakrabarty Worked As a Clown!', *Times of India*, 20 Dec 2010, timesofindia.indiatimes.com/entertainment/bengali/movies/news/Tulsi-Chakrabarty-worked-as-a-clown/articleshow/7126976.cms, accessed on 15 May 2017.

take another bus to Howrah. That would cost another anna. At the most, another anna would be required for him to reach home. Even those three annas, he wanted to save to make ends meet.[8]

In the same interview, Bibhu recounts a sad story about Chakraborty's interaction with Ray when he offered a daily remuneration of ₹100 to the actor. Tulsi Chakraborty refused the amount and requested him to offer lesser pay! He was apprehensive that if the other production houses got to know about the remuneration, he would not get any work in future!

However, Chakraborty's performance bedazzled the audience and the critics. His nuanced growth from a general clerk of a government office who is doubtful, god-fearing and unambitious, to a wealthy man courtesy of the philosopher's stone, was spectacular. Film critic Marie Seton remarked: 'In the whole range of the remarkable performances in Ray's films none surpasses in subtlety of emotional variation that of the late Tulsi Chakraborty as Paresh Dutta. This previously little known actor created the memorable cameo of the pundit-grocer in *Pather Panchali*.'[9] Andrew Robinson, on the other hand, went a step further in his praise—

---

[8]ibid.

[9]Marie Seton, *Portrait of a Director*, Penguin Books India, 2002, p. 274.

'Chakravarti recalls Chaplin at his best. Instead of a moustache he has a pair of eyes as bulbous as a frog's which he opens wide with every emotion known to Man.'[10]

Jahar Roy was another great comedian of the Bengali screen who, along with Bhanu Bandyopadhyay, formed a formidable duo similar to Laurel and Hardy and presented laugh riots in films such as *Bhanu Goenda Jahar Assistant*, *Jamalaye Jibanta Manush*, *Ashi te Asio na*, *Bhanu Pelo Lottery*, *Saare Chuattor* and so on. Bhanu never feature, in any of Ray's films, but Ray did cast Jahar in two films. First, he was the servant in Paresh Dutta's household in *Paras Pathar,* where his role is rather insignificant. Second, he played the evil prime minister in *Goopy Gyne Bagha Byne*. Roy, famous for generating comedy through physical acting, was best suited for the latter role. His voice modulations bring out the guile of the bad man effectively.

Comedy as a genre remains a very distinctive part of Bengali cinema. Ray's comic films demand a special space and mention in his oeuvre, with the inimitable performances of their highly efficient actors.

---

[10]Andrew Robinson, *Satyajit Ray: The Inner Eye*, Rupa and Co, 1990, p. 108.

Satyajit Ray in a reflective mood.
Photo courtesy: Asit Poddar

Top: Satyajit Ray in his study room.
Bottom: Satyajit Ray with wife, Bijoya, and son, Sandip.
Photos courtesy: Asit Poddar

Top: Sarbajaya, Durga and young Apu in *Pather Panchali*.
Bottom: Indir Thakrun and young Durga in *Pather Panchali*.
Photos courtesy: The Society for the Preservation of Satyajit Ray Archives

Top: Sharmila Tagore and Soumitra Chatterjee as Aparna and Apu, respectively, in their debut film *Apur Sansar*.

Bottom: Sharmila Tagore and Soumitra Chatterjee appear together for the last time in *Aranyer Din Ratri*.

Photos courtesy: The Society for the Preservation of Satyajit Ray Archives

Top: Chhabi Biswas as the aristocratic patriarch in *Jalsaghar*.
Bottom: The inimitable Tulsi Chakraborty in *Paras Pathar*.
Photos courtesy: The Society for the Preservation of Satyajit Ray Archives

Top: Rabi Ghosh and Tapen Chatterjee as Bagha and Goopi, respectively, in the iconic *Goopi Gyne Bagha Byne*.

Bottom: Ray's favourite Soumitra Chatterjee as Feluda, the detective, with his associates in *Joy Baba Felunath*.

Photos courtesy: The Society for the Preservation of Satyajit Ray Archives

Top: The 'city hero', Pradip Mukherjee, in *Jana Aranya*
Bottom: The 'city hero', Dhritiman Chatterjee, in *Pratidwandi.*
Photos courtesy: The Society for the Preservation of Satyajit Ray Archives

Top: Dhritiman as the 'villain' with Soumitra Chatterjee in *Ganashatru*.
Bottom: Utpal Dutt as the stranger in Satyajit Ray's last film *Agantuk*.
Photos courtesy: The Society for the Preservation of Satyajit Ray Archives

SOUMITRA CHATTERJEE,
RAY'S BLUE-EYED BOY

On 1 May 1959, a film was released simultaneously in three cinema halls in Calcutta: Rupbani, Aruna and Bharati. It created history probably without anyone understanding the magnum implications of the event. It was *Apur Sansar* (*The World of Apu*), Satyajit Ray's third and final part of his masterpiece, *The Apu Trilogy*. Over the years, the film has influenced generations of audiences—from film-makers to film critics and general cine-goers. It has made it to lists of the 100 greatest movies of all time prepared by different organizations at different points in time. In the Indian context, apart from all these laurels, it also launched two debutants who made shy, yet sublime, entries into Indian cinema. The heroine, Sharmila Tagore, who was in her early teens when she first acted as Aparna in *Apur Sansar,* went on to become one of the leading ladies of Hindi cinema in the '60s and the '70s, occasionally returning to her roots in the Ray films of the '60s. The hero Soumitra Chatterjee, on the other hand, never ventured out of Bengali cinema and remained a regional actor throughout his life—and yet attained international acclaim and a reputation befitting the same. He is the quintessential Bengali, the harbinger of youth, and unlike many other 'heroes' of Indian cinema, he aged gracefully. Acting in fourteen of Ray's feature films, Soumitra shared a rare chemistry with the master film-maker which no other actor could garner—and in the process became the representative face of Satyajit Ray's body of work. Termed as 'Ray's One-man Stock Company' by renowned film author Pauline Kael, Soumitra remained Ray's close associate and shared the same bond with him that one may find between Ingmar Bergman and Max von Sydow or Akira Kurosawa and Toshiro Mifune. On 9 August 1990, during a retrospective of Soumitra Chatterjee's films organized by Cine Central, Calcutta, Satyajit Ray paid tribute to his favourite actor—

> I don't think there is any need to give a certificate to Soumitra. Of my twenty-seven films, Soumitra featured in the main roles in fourteen of them. This itself will prove what trust I have in him and how I value him as an actor. I do know that to the last day of my artist's life, my dependence on him will remain intact.[1]

To Soumitra, this appreciation more valuable than the many awards that he has received in his illustrious career spanning over six decades. However, looking back, the initiation began with disappointment.

---

[1]Amitava Nag, *Beyond Apu: 20 Favourite Film Roles of Soumitra Chatterjee*, Harper Collins India, 2016, p. 138.

THE INITIATION AND APUR SANSAR

Satyajit Ray's *Pather Panchali* (1955) changed the course of Indian cinema completely. Deeply humanist in mood yet existentially real in its rendition, Ray's film soon started to open up new avenues for Indian film-makers, alongside creating a niche for itself with the foreign critics and lovers of cinema. In the mid-50s, Soumitra was a student of literature and wasn't greatly impressed by the medium of cinema before Ray's masterpiece was released. Those days, Soumitra was visiting the doyen of Bengali theatre—Sisir Kumar Bhaduri—and dreaming of becoming a theatre actor under the tutelage of this great master. *Pather Panchali* changed Soumitra's perception of cinema in general and the possibilities of Bengali cinema in particular. So when the news of Ray's plan for a sequel to *Pather Panchali* was released, it drew more than a few eyeballs—including Chatterjee's. Ray was planning to make *Aparajito* (*The Unvanquished*) and needed a slightly grown up Apu for the film. Soumitra recalls,

> One day, when we were sitting in Coffee House, I noticed that my friend Tapan was signaling to someone on the footpath while trying to engage me in a discussion. When I asked what he was up to, he said, 'That's a friend of mine who works in

Satyajit Ray's unit. They are looking for someone to play Apu in *Aparajito*. Would you be willing to go and meet Mr Ray once?' Needless to say I was ready, and went to Mr Ray's house with Tapan's friend. The moment I entered Mr Ray's room he told me, 'Oh-ho, you are a bit taller than my conception of Apu.' I was amazed by his single-minded focus on the subject. Evidently he was so immersed in the film that this was what he said to me at our very first meeting! He then talked to me in a general way, asking what I did, etc. But I was not cast as Apu in *Aparajito!*[2]

That left Soumitra slightly disappointed even though he was more into theatre in those days. However, he soon got a call from Ray. He recollects,

When Manik-da (Satyajit Ray's pet name) was making *Paras Pathar* and *Jalsaghar*, I went down with chickenpox. After I recovered he summoned me once again, and I went to his house. He said, 'Let's see, they told me that there are some scars on your face but I see that it's not too bad. Good. Are you interested in acting?' I nodded. He asked if I had ever acted before. I told him about my

---

[2]ibid., pp. 1–2.

association with Sisir Bhaduri. Mr Ray said, 'I am about to make the third part of *The Apu trilogy* and I would like to cast you but I will need voice and camera tests. Do keep in touch with me.' I was not sure at that point in time which role he had in mind for me, but I started visiting the studio more often. I realized much later that he did all this to put me at ease, and make me less self-conscious before the camera. As a matter of fact he had already chosen me (for the role) before doing these tests, and the tests were just a formality. One day I was on the sets watching him shoot, as I often did. The film was *Jalsaghar*, and Chhabi Biswas, the legendary actor, was on the floor. Mr Ray introduced me to him, saying, 'This is Soumitra Chatterjee. He is playing Apu in my next film.' My head started reeling. I wanted to run out and shout to everyone, 'Satyajit Ray has chosen me for Apu! Satyajit Ray has chosen me!' I came to know much later that he had decided to make the third part of *The Apu Trilogy* when he first saw me![3]

Soumitra Chatterjee first stood in front of the rolling camera on 9 August 1958, and this association with his mentor, Satyajit Ray, remained until the latter's death

---

[3]ibid., pp. 2–3

in 1992. Soumitra's Apu became an instant hit amongst the Bengali youth, who were wandering in search of a role model—a romantic who is an extension of nature. Uttam Kumar was already a matinee idol by then and a section of educated middle-class Bengali men took to Soumitra instantly, making him almost a screen rival to Uttam, who had already acted in more than fifty films by then. Uttam remained the biggest star of Bengali cinema and Soumitra continued to acquire his own acting laurels alongside. Film critics liked Soumitra's Apu as an iconic romantic youth with his innocent charm and natural ebullience as *The Times* reviewer referred to him as the 'Biblical lesson (Luke 10:8)— The Children of Light'. In her seminal book on Satyajit Ray, *Portrait of a Director*, Marie Seton comments, 'In portraying Apu, Soumitra Chatterjee felt Apu to be the image of the contemporary Indian man in the process of becoming modern... He found half of himself in Apu.'[4]

RISE TO STARDOM—THE CLASSICAL '60s

The decade of the '60s happens to be a glorious period for Bengali cinema. In the previous decade, the Uttam—

---

[4]Marie Seton, *Portrait of a Director*, Penguin Books India, 2002, pp. 107–10.

Suchitra duo rocked the Bengali screen and all the prominent directors along side Ray, including Ritwik Ghatak, Mrinal Sen, Tapan Sinha, Ajoy Kar, Asit Sen and a few others, had already arrived by then. The '60s was a decade of reconciliation of the earlier times and for extending the creative pursuits further. As an actor, Soumitra benefitted the most as he acted in six Ray films, two Tapan Sinha films, three Mrinal Sen films, three Asit Sen films and four films of Ajoy Kar during that period. Soumitra's second film in his career was *Devi* by Satyajit Ray, where he plays Umaprasad, pairing again with Sharmila Tagore as Doyamoyee. The film plays on religious superstition and how a young bride falls prey to it. Soumitra, as the helpless husband, brings out the pathos and angst of a society and of a time when, within the confines of patriarchy, contrary voices were muted and subdued.

After *Devi*, Soumitra acted in *Kshudita Pashan* by Tapan Sinha, another stalwart, before returning to a Ray film as the hero of *Samapti*, the third part of *Teen Kanya* (1961). Incidentally, *Samapti* introduced Aparna Sen, another luminary of Indian cinema, who would later pair up with Soumitra to form a bankable star-couple in commercial Bengali cinema of the '60s and the '70s. *Samapti* belongs to the humour genre and Soumitra, in a sense, seemed to have extended his Apu image to the role of Amulya in *Samapti.* Soumitra recollects,

> I was young, when it is natural to be both foolish and stubborn, and that (the similarity between myself and Amulya) strikes me as amusing at this stage of my life. Amulya is made to carry a picture of Napoleon, whom he hero worships, but he is really a typical Bengali youth! I approached the character from that perspective. We all go through a phase when we take ourselves too seriously, and try to appear more dignified than we are. This is a (good) example of comedy.[5]

Veteran director Shyam Benegal, whose reverence for Ray is well known, adds:

> Soumitra Chatterjee as the young eligible bachelor, by turns awkward, shy and slightly out of place, gave an extraordinarily nuanced performance... Highly skilled actor that he is, he successfully disguises the immense effort that goes into the creation of his role. Soumitra Chatterjee's performance can be compared to a fine Persian carpet, subtle and exquisite. It is only when you turn to look at the back of the carpet do

---

[5]Amitava Nag, *Beyond Apu: 20 Favourite film roles of Soumitra Chatterjee*, Harper Collins India, 2016, p. 11.

you see the intricate weave that has gone into its making.[6]

The next year, Soumitra returned as a Rajput taxi driver in Ray's *Abhijan*, which also had Waheeda Rehman playing his ladylove. The film was originally planned to be directed by a first-time director who approached Ray for the screenplay. Bijoy Chatterjee, who wished to direct the film and planned to cast Uttam Kumar as the taxi driver, soon backed out, making Ray the director. Ray changed the cast and had Soumitra play Narsingh. This was indeed challenging for Soumitra since till then his image was that of a romantic Bengali who is soft spoken, dreamy and draped in an innocuous charm. Possibly to change his naturally elegant handsomeness, Ray made Soumitra sport a rugged look with long hair and a tough beard. Soumitra grabbed the chauvinist role with both hands and delivered with aplomb by changing his body language and also by mixing up his predominantly Bengali dialogue with broken Hindi words. It made Narsingh more convincing and stamped Soumitra as a remarkably versatile actor.

In 1964, Ray directed *Charulata* based on Rabindranath Tagore's masterful short story *Nastaneer*. Set in the latter part of nineteenth century Bengal, the film follows

---

[6]ibid., p. 12.

three characters bound in a triangular love-story in an affluent middle-class home. Madhabi Mukherjee as Charulata and Soumitra Chatterjee as Amal along with Sailen Mukherjee as Bhupati, Charu's husband, form the three sides of this love-triangle. Amal resembled a young Tagore—and who else in Bengali cinema at that time could play him to the core but Soumitra? Amal has an inner radiance similar to Apu's but whereas for Apu, the journey was mostly an individualistic one, Amal's positioning was more complex within the mesh of love and conflict. Andrew Robinson observes, 'As Amal, Soumitra Chatterjee fits his role brilliantly too, and gives his finest performance in the fourteen films by Ray in which he appears, full of verve and wit.'[7] Soumitra did something unique to play Amal—he changed his Bengali handwriting for good. Ray insisted that Amal's handwriting should be pre-Tagorean in style and the film should have several close-up shots of Amal's writing. Ray provided Soumitra with several texts and explained how the alphabets would look like. After six months of diligent practice, Chatterjee could successfully change his style of writing completely—at the age of twenty-seven!

The very next year, Satyajit Ray repeated Soumitra

---

[7]Andrew Robinson, *Satyajit Ray: The Inner Eye*, Rupa and Co, 1990, p. 162.

and Madhabi in *Kapurush* (the second part of the two-segment film *Kapurush-o-Mahapurush*), which translates to '*coward*'. Interestingly, none of the Soumitra–Madhabi starrers, even the ones not by Ray, happened to end on a happy note. *Kapurush*, like *Charulata,* is a love triangle where Amitava (played by Soumitra) recoils from the scene, much like Amal. However, Amal's radical brilliance illuminates every scene, endearing him to the audience, whereas Amitava seems to be a selfish loser who is self-absorbed and somewhat conceited.

Soumitra's last film with Ray in the '60s happens to be *Aranyer Din Ratri* (*Days and Nights in the Forest*) in 1969. *Aranyer Din Ratri* is an important milestone in Ray's oeuvre since he subsequently moved on to his more political and certainly polemical Calcutta Trilogy (*Pratidwandi, Seemabaddha* and *Jana Aranya*). The film is significant for Ray's classical and lyrical approach to a modern theme, which resonated with the Western audience much more than it did with its Indian counterpart. For Soumitra the film remains equally important, since afterwards he played different central 'characters' in Ray's films, but not the protagonist who would serve as the director's alter ego. As Ashim, the leader of the quartet, who works in a corporate firm and is well paid, Soumitra exuded the arrogance expected of the role—vacuous and pretentious. As the film progresses, his relation with Aparna (played again by Sharmila Tagore and bearing the same name as Apu's bride in *Apur Sansar!*) reveals his inner, weak emotional side. Soumitra brings out the inner conflict with ease, transitioning from a confident individual to a deeply wounded and unsure one whose self-confidence has been dealt a serious blow by Aparna's simple effervescence. Sharmila Tagore didn't appear with Soumitra in any other Ray film after this one. She comments, 'This was one of the really good films of Manik-da, through which he tried to understand the present generation. I think Soumitra played the character very well—he is confident yet vulnerable. In the beginning he is cocky but then as the film progresses, the character becomes more human and I think he played it to perfection.'[8]

CHARACTER ROLES—THE LAST SEVEN

After *Aranyer Din Ratri*, Satyajit Ray made *Pratidwandi* (1970) and had Dhritiman Chatterjee play Siddhartha, the protagonist. Soumitra, hence, featured seven more times in Ray's films, and apart from *Ganashatru* (1990), he was never the 'voice' or the 'conscience' of the director even though he played central characters

---

[8]Amitava Nag, *Beyond Apu: 20 Favourite Film Roles of Soumitra Chatterjee*, Harper Collins India, 2016, pp. 57–58.

in almost all of these seven films. Soumitra plays the priest Gangacharan in *Ashani Sanket* (*Distant Thunder*), in 1973—a film which is important to him as an actor since here again, like *Abhijan*, he plays a character whose social and economic condition is far removed from his own. Shot in rural Bengal against the backdrop of the Bengal Famine of 1943, the film won the Golden Bear for Best Film at the Berlin International Film Festival in 1973. Soumitra worked hard for the role, accompanying the director during recce and observing the rural people of Bengal. He would draw their postures while sitting, standing and walking, and use them in his authentic portrayal of a village priest. As he did for *Apur Sansar*, for *Ashani Sanket*, Soumitra engaged himself in detailed note-work on the character, trying to eke out background information that was absent in the script. The result was stupendous and drew rave reviews from critics.

Satyajit Ray was an unparalleled genius. Apart from being an excellent illustrator and painter alongside his film-making prowess, he also revived publication of *Sandesh*, a unique children's literary magazine in 1961. For *Sandesh*, Satyajit started writing stories for children, which soon became immensely popular. In 1965, Ray introduced Feluda, a detective who is Bengali to the core yet international in his vision. Feluda soon became extremely popular amongst children and young adults, turning him into a cult figure and, now, a cultural icon. During his tenure, Ray made two films based on the Feluda stories—*Sonar Kella* in 1974 and *Joy Baba Felunath* in 1979. Soumitra had a liking for Felu right from the start and had always felt that Ray seemed to have modelled Felu on himself—'I always felt that the character of Felu was essentially a projection of Satyajit Ray himself, reflecting his thirst for knowledge and his insatiable curiosity about everything.'[9] Ray, who did all the illustrations for all his stories and books himself, would joke that many people told him that the drawing of Felu must have been modelled on Soumitra. After *Sonar Kella*, Ray purposely illustrated Felu with Soumitra in mind so that any possible confusion was resolved. For Soumitra, playing Felu was exciting since 'till that time I had not acted in a children's film. My own children were young then and knowing that they would enjoy the Felu-da films gave me a lot of pleasure.'[10]

Since Felu is a detective who relies heavily on his cerebral functions rather than action like most Western sleuths, Soumitra used his eyes to great effect to bring forth the sharpness inherent in the character. Amongst all the characters that Soumitra played in Ray's cinema, Felu is probably amongst the top three most popular

[9] ibid., p. 76.
[10] ibid.

ones, along with Apu and Amal. Felu is still revered and almost worshipped by teens, and his popularity is so intense that there have been multiple Felu films made by Sandip Ray with two different actors playing Felu. Yet, the quintessential Felu remains Soumitra, whose blending of intellect and intelligence gave his version a rare, unmatched edge.

Soumitra next played Udayan, a village schoolteacher on exile who comes to the rescue of Goopy and Bagha in *Hirak Rajar Deshe*, a film which is hailed as a direct criticism of the contemporary government and its regimented vision, and remains an important satire in Indian cinema.

Ray's next full-length feature was *Ghare Baire* (1984), which remains important on multiple accounts. Based on Tagore's novel and bearing a resemblance to *Charulata* in being a triangular love story, this is one film that Ray wanted to make even before he directed *Pather Panchali*. For the next three decades, Satyajit ruminated on making it and postponed again and again. Finally, he started shooting the film in December 1982, but stopped in 1983 following his massive heart attack. Sandip Ray finally completed the film under Ray's guidance. The film is also important since this is one of the rare occasions where there is a clear 'villain' in a Ray film in the form of Sandip (played by Soumitra), pitted against the more innocent and gullible 'hero' Nikhilesh (played by Victor Banerjee). Soumitra loved playing the villain since Sandip's character has more shades in his palette than Nikhilesh's. However, initially when Ray thought of making *Ghare Baire* in the '60s, he had planned to cast Soumitra as Nikhilesh. Soumitra observes,

> Manik-da initially used to tell me that I would do Nikhilesh. This is shortly after *Apur Sansar*... Sometime later he began saying I would play either Nikhilesh or Sandip, based on the availability of the other actor. But much before he actually made *Ghare Baire* he decided to cast me as Sandip and started looking for an actor to play Nikhilesh.[11]

Sandip was a nationalist leader and an eloquent speaker. This is why Ray wanted Soumitra to play the role given the latter's refined diction, which very few Bengali actors possessed at that time. Also, Soumitra's romantic image helped lend plausibility to Bimala's attraction towards him in spite of her husband Nikhilesh being an epitome of virtue. Like most of his crucial roles, as Sandip, too, Soumitra uses his expressive face and emotive eyes to shift from the

---

[11]ibid., p. 92.

initial acquaintance with Bimala to his cunning and deceitful manipulations and finally to his amorous adventures. *Ghare Baire*'s Sandip remains a character who is despicable yet suave, and Soumitra plays him with great artistic sensibilities.

Soumitra eventually acted in two of Ray's last three films—*Ganashatru* (1990) and *Shakha Proshakha* (1992). In *Ganashatru,* based on Henrik Ibsen's powerful *An Enemy of the People,* Soumitra plays the protagonist Doctor Gupta. The film had its cinematic punches but failed to live up to Ray's standards both aesthetically and philosophically. Soumitra essays the role of a disillusioned doctor to perfection—someone who stands for his beliefs even when the society around him disintegrates and takes up arms against him. Finally, after the 60s, Soumitra again plays a character who reflects the director's inner turmoil and acts as an extension of his creator. In *Shakha Proshakha,* Soumitra plays Prashanta, a deranged second son of a successful industrialist whose other three sons visit them on the latter's seventieth birthday. Like *Ganashatru, Shakha Proshakha* also had great possibilities, but ultimately failed, probably due to Ray's failing health.

Soumitra remained an integral part of Ray's cinema. No discussion on Ray's films is complete without a reference to Soumitra Chatterjee; he is that indispensable. This marks his tremendous contribution and reflects the camaraderie between the actor and the director. Perhaps Shyam Benegal summed up the relation best in his short incisive account:

> Soumitra Chatterjee is an exceptional discovery of Satyajt Ray. From *Apur Sansar* to the last day of his life, Soumitra Chatterjee was in Ray's creative mind. Is Satyajit babu's magnified artistic world fully radiant without Soumitra? It will be a futile exercise to think of a substitute for Soumitra Chatterjee who portrayed so many tough and multi-dimensional characters on celluloid. He did not get any assistance from the sophisticated technology and unique camera of Hollywood; he had to work within a very limited technical support. Soumitra babu could cover many technical flaws with his magic of acting. What is most striking about Soumitra babu is his sensitivity, the unfading asset of a born actor. Charlie Chaplin, Toshiro Mifune, Gerard Depardieu were certainly the sensitive actors who dominated the world of cinema with their brilliance. The contemporary scenario helped them a lot to develop their sensitive feelings to a great extent. But in case of Soumitra Chatterjee

there was no easy grammar of sensitive acting, he had to frame everything on his own. From the highly imaginative Apu he became a realistic Apu and in both the cases sensitivity was very much dominated, of course with different colours. But it was really difficult to bridge the gap and Soumitra did the job without any stress and strain... His Sandeep in *Ghare Baire* and Prasanta in *Shakha Proshakha* were also two characterizations in which Soumitra babu's inherent qualities to portray all types of character found ample vibrant expressions.[12]

---

[12]ibid., p. 139.

'VILLAINS BORE ME'

In one of his interviews, Ray had categorically mentioned that villains, in general, bored him. What he probably meant was the common depiction of an all-evil person in popular culture, including mainstream cinema and the literature, globally. For him, human beings were more ambivalent and less monochromatic. Delivering the Satyajit Ray Memorial Lecture in Kolkata, in 2009, Javed Akhtar, the noted lyricist of Hindi cinema remarked on Ray's negative characters—'His characters only had negative shades. They were people trapped in their own thinking and beliefs. While Hindi films have ferocious villains who only evoked hatred, you actually felt sad for Ray's negative characters. Such was the sensitivity of the man.'[1] It is indeed difficult to find many Ray characters who have substantial screen time and yet turn out to be completely villainous in their actions. Even smaller roles with negative traits have a silver lining to arouse sensitivity for them. For example, Umapada, the brother of Charu in *Charulata*. He breaks Bhupati's trust in a single move, though he had prepared for it over time. There is an apparent reason for his act of dishonesty, may seem plausible in a sense even if unsupportable. In Ray's early films, which are romantic

---

[1]Andrew Robinson, *The Apu Trilogy: Satyajit Ray and the Making of an Epic*, I. B. Tauris & Co Ltd, 2011, p. 165.

in nature and classical in form, the negative characters rarely appear.

One of the earliest negative roles in a Ray film was Nanda Babu's in the second part of *The Apu Trilogy*, *Aparajito*.

> From the top of the frame now appear two feet clad in shiny new pumps—obviously Nanda Babu's. One of the pumps prods one of the skinny little creatures, not so much because it is in the way, but out of casual cruelty typical of its owner. That is all... Sarbajaya's defencelessness has been crystallized... His face unseen Nanda Babu slips off his pumps, crosses the threshold, and takes a few steps, his fingers splayed out and trembling with sexual excitement. 'Bouthan', he says in a low voice, 'are you making pan?'... Sarbajaya, with blind instinct, threatens Nanda Babu with a kitchen blade, and he beats a hasty retreat.[2]

The role is played by Charuprakash Ghosh, who was a theatre actor and activist associated with the Gana Natya Sangha. Ray repeated Ghosh in two more films. In *Abhijan*, Ghosh plays Sukhanram, the uncouth Marwari businessman. Charuprakash's acting talent was revealed

---

[2]ibid., pp. 116–17.

fully in Sukhanram. His dialogue delivery, that was a mixture of broken Bengali and the ubiquitous greed conveyed through his facial expression, was stunning. Sukhanram ran a smuggling business and appeared to be helping Narsingh, the taxi driver, who had fallen into hard times. Quite cunningly, Sukhanram would use Narsingh as a pawn in his game plan and make use of the latter's helplessness and love for his car to induct him into his smuggling racket. Charuprakash's stoic mien was used to portray his character's negative vibes. In Ray's films, the protagonists primarily reflect what the upper-caste Brahmins look like. From his favourites including Soumitra Chatterjee, Sharmila Tagore, Madhabi Mukherjee to even the heroes of his later films like Pradip Mukherjee, Dhritiman Chatterjee and Dipankar De, all of them bear a fair-skinned, sharp-featured semblance. The ones who are not, like Rabi Ghosh or Santosh Dutta or even the legendary Utpal Dutt, are there either for comic relief or to portray grotesque negative characters. Hence, it is no coincidence to find Charuprakash Ghosh being repeated again by Satyajit Ray in *Mahapurush,* of his couplet *Kapurush-o-Mahapurush.* Based on noted satirist Rajsekhar Basu's popular short story *Birinchibaba,* the film depicts a god-man who claims to be ageless. His long talks touch upon his associations with Plato,

Gautama Buddha, teaching Einstein the basics of relativity and what not! Filmed in a comic vein keeping the satire intact, Ray's sly, understated jibing at the blind religious beliefs of the masses couldn't be ignored. Charuprakash Ghosh probably gave his best performance as Birinchibaba. The greed that is abundant in Sukhanram is not as palpable here. He sports a veneer that falls off only in front of his close aide (played marvelously by Rabi Ghosh), and later at the end, when his antics are revealed and he has to leave the place. Charuprakash Ghosh as the charlatan remains an important character in Ray's oeuvre— someone who is continuously referred to in serious discussions as well as in popular culture and social parody snippets.

Portraying a negative character in the guise of comedy was something Ray definitely delved in consciously. Perhaps in this way, he could concentrate on the evil in society that he wanted to decry instead of blaming an individual as a villain. In *Goopy Gyne Bagha Byne*, Jahar Roy plays the crooked prime minister of Halla, who vitiates the mind of the King of Halla, making him go to war against the kingdom of Shundi ruled by the king's brother. The minister is depicted as a fat man, full of himself—his greed is almost lascivious. His main aide is a mysterious magician who casts a spell that makes all the people in the kingdom of Shundi dumb. He also poisons the King of Halla with a magic potion, which incapacitates the latter for large periods of time. The remaining time the king is intoxicated to become vigorous and violent, only to lose his virility soon afterwards.

Jahar Roy was one of the most celebrated comedians of Bengali cinema. In this role, Ray made him mix his comic mannerisms, keeping his slyness intact. Roy was adept enough to portray the character to the core. In one deft scene, we find him gobbling a big plate full of chicken pieces in front of a low-ranked spy in his army who is ill-fed and starving. The depravity of the character is thus completely established.

Ray's sublime political slant, which becomes more pronounced and direct with his *Calcutta Trilogy,* has its seeds in *Goopy Gyne Bagha Byne.* In one scene, the prime minister threatens to behead Goopy and Bagha if they repeat a song that had melted the king's heart. This depiction of authoritative governance that throttles the common citizen and robs them of their basic and natural instincts resonates in today's world. Ray continued the same with more vigour in the sequel, *Hirak Rajar Deshe.* In *Goopy Gyne Bagha Byne,* Ray's message was more of an anti-war statement, as the duo sings near the end of the film—'O the soldiers of Halla, On bloody wars no nation thrives, So what are you fighting for'. In the sequel, filmed in 1980, Ray's stance was firmly rooted to the situation of the country that he had witnessed and assessed for a decade. The Indian Emergency, dismantling the fabric of rational tolerance and free speech for twenty-one months between 1975 and 1977, had its definite representation in *Hirak Rajar Deshe*. Here, the King himself is genuinely oppressive, as if the prime minister of Halla has been reincarnated with more bile. Ray put his faith in Utpal Dutt for the role of the King of Hirak Rajya (meaning the kingdom of diamonds). Dutt was also a prominent actor in cinema, and received the National Film Award for Best Actor in 1970 for his profoundly somber yet sublimely light representation of a fifty-odd years old dedicated civil servant in Mrinal Sen's *Bhuvan Shome*. Apart from several Bengali films where he played comic and villainous roles with equal finesse, Dutt left his mark on Hindi cinema as well. On the one hand, he is the despicable villain opposite Amitabh Bachchan in *The Great Gambler* and *Inquilaab* or Uttam Kumar in *Amanush,* on the other, he is the lovable yet comic Bhawani Shankar in *Golmaal* and *Naram Garam,* the police officer in *Rang Birangi* or the simple, innocent widower Kailash Pati in *Kissi Se Na Kehna.* Dutt also featured in significant roles in Mrinal Sen's *Chorus* and *Calcutta 71* and Ritwik Ghatak's last film

Jukti Takko aar Gappo. In fact, his first Ray film was *Jana Aranya* in 1976, although his role as Bisu da was a small one. In *Hirak Rajar Deshe*, Utpal Dutt brings life to his character with a rare authenticity. An avowed communist throughout his life, Dutt had already written, directed and staged plays in the '70s which were all extremely popular and supremely political, including *Dusswapner Nagari* (*City of Nightmares*) and *Ebaar Rajar Pala* (*Now It is the King's Turn*). These, along with *Barricade,* were banned by the Congress Government in the '70s and during the national Emergency. Dutt's creativity mingled with his political ideology so effortlessly that he could deliver a character so despicable with such strong shades. His sense of Marxism was so ingrained and pure that he could comment thus on Ray's detractors, who would condemn Ray as a bourgeois:

> Why, he has handled socio-political themes in most striking ways. His *Devi* uprooted superstitions, fashionably called religion in this country. People who talk Marxism wouldn't dare touch that kind of a dynamite. Mr Ray, who is not a demonstrator, who is silent at all the critical moments of politics, has made that revolutionary film.[3]

---

[3]Utpal Dutt Interview, 'The Genius of Satyajit Ray Issue', *Frontline* magazine, 20 December 1991, p. 85.

Dutt went on to explain his appreciation of Ray:

> The quality of restraint that Ray brought into
> Indian cinema does not in any way lessen the
> force of the depiction. I have never seen a more
> passionate scene than the one in *Pather Panchali*
> when the father hears that his girl is dead. He
> screams at the sky in despair. Charulata throws
> herself on the bed and weeps for the man she
> loves. Ray knows that passion is not cheap. He
> uses it with intensity but only where and when it is
> necessary.[4]

Like the prime minister in *Goopy Gyne Bagha Byne,*
the King in *Hirak Rajar Deshe,* too, doesn't receive any
salvation. Ray is merciless when he points his fingers at
the ruling powers that dictate and regulate the lives of
the masses.

Before *Hirak Rajar Deshe* and after *Jana Aranya,* Dutt
acted in only one Ray film as the meticulous villain
Maganlal Meghraj in *Joy Baba Felunath*—the last film in
the Feluda series. Feluda was Ray's own literary creation
and even fifty years later, (the first Feluda story, *Feludar
Goenda Giri,* was published in *Sandesh* in 1965), he is still
as popular as he used to be. In one of his later stories,

---

[4]ibid., pp. 89–90.

Feluda admits that the most heinous villain he has ever encountered in his career is Maganlal Meghraj, whom he came across more than once—the first time being in *Joy Baba Felunath*. When Ray decided to transform this Feluda story into a film, he chose Utpal Dutt to play the non-Bengali businessman villain. Dutt, who like Charuprakash Ghosh in *Abhijan* mixes his Hindi with occasional accented Bengali, brings in the right tinge for an immensely successful portrayal. Maganlal is indeed formidable, and halfway into the film, we find him inviting Feluda and his associates to his den and humiliating him wholly. Utpal Dutt gave a staggering performance as Maganlal with his bulbous eyes, which were cold and terrifying. He had by then played the villain in many a film—Bengali and Hindi. Yet, Maganlal is unique in the way he catapulted the 'villain' from being physically abrasive to someone more refined, whose intelligence is capable of giving the sleuth a run for his money. Dutt appeared as Maganlal again in Sandip Ray's Television series *Kissa Kathmandu Ka* made in Hindi for Doordarshan in the mid-80s, with Sashi Kapoor playing Feluda.

Utpal Dutt's last appearance in a Ray film is incidentally Ray's last work as well—*Agantuk*. The film, which is the culmination of Ray's philosophical quest and yet lacking his subtle brilliance, is remembered also for an ageing Dutt's riveting performance. Soumitra Chatterjee wanted to play the role of Manmohan in *Agantuk*. In a personal interview he told me, 'I was very keen to play Manmohan in his last film *Agantuk* as well which was later played by Utpal Dutt.' However, Ray didn't agree. Chatterjee said,

> Manik-da told me 'your image will make the audience believe that this stranger cannot be anything but a nice, honest person. But I want to have some suspense that's why the person needs to be a little grotesque in his mannerisms,' I had nothing more to tell him but accept.[5]

Manmohan comes across an indifferent man in the beginning, someone who has a mysterious past, but he slowly turns out to be that messiah who puts us—the middle-class—in front of a mirror. This was quite a different role for Dutt, who passed away a couple of years later. Manmohan is neither his trademark villain, nor his quintessential comic character. He has multiple shades with less theatricality. In his trademark gentle tirade, Ray chides at the contributions

---

[5]'The Elusive Roles of Ray's Man Friday', *The Hindu*, 24 January 2016, https://www.thehindu.com/news/cities/mumbai/The-elusive-roles-of-Ray%E2%80%99s-Man-Friday/article14017550.ece, accessed on 22 November 2018.

of modern civilization through Manmohan when the latter amusingly comments that the longest word in the first edition of the Oxford English Dictionary is 'floccinaucinihilipilification'—such a long word to mean 'something of little of no value'! In his last film, this may be Ray's own way of reflecting on his own life, that has come a full circle, and towards the life of humans in general. The film in a sense sums up Ray's intrinsic dichotomy between tradition and modernity throughout most of his films.

Amongst all these films, if Maganlal is an outright 'villain', the only other character close to him is Sandip in *Ghare Baire,* based on Rabindranth Tagore's novel. Chidananda Dasgupta says,

> In the oeuvre of Satyajit Ray, *Ghare Baire* will come to occupy a very special place. He had finally grown out of the Apu mold... For the first time he has a villain; and this itself marks a sea change. Even the pimping PRO of *Jana Aranya* (Rabi Ghosh) and the Madam (Padma Devi) of the whorehouse were not wholly evil; their sparkling humour gave them a human warmth... And now in *Ghare Baire,* when Sandip bares his fangs from behind a polite mask, the villain at last emerges in Ray's work... Soumitra Chatterjee, the archetypal innocent of

Ray's cinema, now gives off certain vibrations of villainy.[6]

The choice of Soumitra was an interesting one. Ray had mentioned to Soumitra his wish to make this film for quite a long time. He initially chose Soumitra as Nikhilesh when the actor was young, but as the possibility of filming *Ghare Baire* kept being deferred, he made up his mind to cast Soumitra as Sandip. Soumitra, later, came to know from Ray's family why Ray chose him to play Sandip:

> He had said, 'Sandip has quite a few long speeches which Soumitra will be able to deliver. Nikhilesh is handsome, upright, and a desirable husband for any wife. The question is, why would Bimala be attracted to Sandip? It is his oratory skills, his dynamism and finesse which draws Bimala to Sandip. I can't find any other actor here whose diction is as good. Add to this Soumitra's romantic image, which would make Bimala's infatuation in the film much more plausible.'...
>
> There is a long speech the first time Sandip comes on screen. While handing me the script, Manik-da asked me to memorize it. It was planned

---

[6]Chidananda Dasgupta, *The Cinema of Satyajit Ray*, National Book Trust, India, 2003, pp. 127–28.

as a single take and hence I would have to deliver it at one go. Later, however, the shot was cut into two-three to show Bimala's reactions and I was not required to deliver the whole speech in one take. But during dubbing, I had the entire speech perfect. Manik-da appreciated that a lot. I still treasure that memory.[7]

Sandip is the intelligent 'bad' man—much different from Maganlal in his shrewdness. He has the façade of an idealist revolutionary who publicly burns down European goods so that 'Swadeshi' products can be used, but smokes foreign cigarettes, eyes Bimala—his close friend's wife—and in the end escapes after putting the Sukhsayar estate ruled by Nikhilesh to communal flames. Soumitra's Sandip has a subtle nuance, which flits from animal instinct to intelligent and intellectual speeches to formidable singing talent—enough to sweep a woman off her feet. *Ghare Baire* would remind one of Ray's earlier *Charulata* (another Tagore adaptation) where there was a love triangle as well. It was Soumitra who was the home wrecker in both cases, but the purity of the love triangle in *Charulata* is degraded to a level in *Ghare Baire*, which is marred by greed and lust. Ray's

---

[7]Amitava Nag, *Beyond Apu: 20 Favourite Film Roles of Soumitra Chatterjee*, Harper Collins India, 2016, p. 93.

romantic vision of life, it seems, is unsettled—if not lost. The noble soul of Amal is lost forever in the decadent one of a 'villain'—Sandip.

UTTAM KUMAR, THE MAHANAYAK

The first real surge of film-making lapped on the shores of Calcutta (as the city was referred to at that time) with the formation of the New Theatres studio on 10 February 1931. The biggest hit of New Theatres happened to be the 1935 film *Devdas,* starring and directed by Pramathesh Barua. *Devdas* was a major box-office success and catapulted Barua to stardom almost overnight. In that early phase of Bengali cinema, Barua was the brightest star, who swept a generation of cine-goers with his distinct charm and, along with Kanan Devi, created a rare luminance on screen. With the Indian Independence in 1947 came the Partition of Bengal and the market for Bengali films suddenly declined. The economic decline of West Bengal dented New Theatres' finances and hopes. The luminaries of New Theatres had already started to waver and many of them, including Bimal Roy, moved to Bombay in search of greener pastures. Millions of refugees from East Pakistan flocked the streets of Calcutta and migrated to other eastern states of Independent India (viz. Assam, Tripura and Meghalaya), and the studio system of Calcutta died an unceremonious death. In this new decade of Independent India, the wounded Bengali hoped for a new sunshine and needed some solace to recuperate from their loss—the physical home and the mental abode. They were not disappointed, and in the two decades that followed, Bengal's cultural spectrum broadened through superlative films, insightful literature and enigmatic theatre productions.

EMERGENCE OF THE STAR COUPLE

Pramathesh Barua passed away in 1951, and with his demise, the Bengali cinema suddenly found itself without a bankable hero. Asit Baran was there, and so were Durgadas and Dhiraj Bhattacharya. However, none of them had the screen presence to sweep the audience off their feet in one film after an other. *Basu Paribar*, directed by Nirmal Dey and released in 1952, is an extremely important film when looked at retrospectively. This is not only because the director went on to make *Saare Chuattor* (1953), a film which till date remains one of the finest comedy films in Bengali, but more importantly, it had a hero who looked assured and raised the potential to fill the vacuum left by Barua. The hero, whose screen name was Uttam Kumar, played the role of the eldest brother of the Basu family who ensured that his near ones are financially secured. Ironically, for almost three decades since then, Uttam Kumar played this role in the context of the Bengali film industry and remained its most bankable star till date. Interestingly, the film also had two versatile actresses who have distinct places in the history of Bengali cinema. Sabitri Chatterjee, who was later cast with Uttam as the heroine in quite a few films, acted in a minor role in *Basu Paribar*. Supriya Choudhury (nee Banerjee) debuted in *Basu Paribar* in the role of Sujata, Uttam's sister. Supriya Devi went on to live-in with Uttam Kumar after ten years in 1963 till Uttam's passing away in 1980, and the two remained another 'hit' pair throughout the '60s and the '70s.

After the success of *Basu Paribar*, Nirmal Dey cast Uttam in his next film, *Saare Chuattor,* the following year. In *Saare Chuattor,* Uttam was paired with Suchitra Sen who had only one released film to her credit until then. *Saare Chuattor*, which was a sold-out comedy, had the leading comedians of Bengal sharing the screen— from Tulsi Chakraborty to Bhanu Bandyopadhyay and Jahar Roy to Nabadwip Halder. For both Uttam and Suchitra, this impish entry was a big success but this success cannot only be attributed to their star quotient. The duo was cast again in 1954 in *Ora Thake Odhare,* which seemed to have taken a leaf out of *Saare Chuattor*. The runaway success of the film ensured that the couple had been accepted by an audience hungry to behold a new romantic onscreen pair after the heady days of Barua and Kanan Devi. In 1954,

Uttam went on to act in six films with Suchitra, the same number he shared with another leading lady of the decade—Sabitri Chatterjee. The biggest hit of 1954 was Agradoot's *Agni Pariksha*. This is the first film of Suchitra and Uttam where both their names appear as the first names in their respective title cards, indicating the trend of their popularity—a phenomenon which never ceased till their last film together. One of the highlights of the films of Suchitra and Uttam is the natural sparkle of the heroine—a model which fit Suchitra better than any other heroine of her time like Sabitri or Supriya. This portrayal of the self-reliant, modern and smart woman is a distinct departure from the earlier generic portrayal of women on the Bengali screen. It has to be borne in mind that the 50's represent the first decade of Independent India, and the aspirations and anxieties of the youth were markedly different from their predecessors. In many ways, they were fuelled by Nehru's dream of a modern nation, which, among other characteristics, had broken free from the constricting customary social laws and was eager to shape its identity in terms of individual choices. Central to this dream was the figure of the romantic couple—modern, yet not excessively westernized, who had the courage to challenge traditional norms of family structure, often go against patriarchal strictures, and find a haven in their togetherness. The films of Suchitra and Uttam seem to embody such a potential as a couple more than any other on-screen couple of Bengali cinema at that time.

In the '50s, Suchitra and Uttam acted in twenty-two films—apart from those mentioned above—*Sadanander Mela* (1954), *Sapmochan* (1955), *Sabar Uparey* (1955), *Ekti Raat* (1956), *Trijama* (1956), *Sagarika* (1956) *Shilpi* (1956), *Harano Sur* (1957), *Jiban Trishna* (1957), *Indrani* (1958), *Suryatoron* (1958) and *Chawa Pawa* (1959), to name some. Most of these films were stupendous successes and had the Bengali audience hooked on the magic of their screen presence. The screenplays of these films, often written quite exclusively with the star pair in mind, had several elements that satisfied the deep, unconscious longing of its audience for a certain kind of romance, one that involved a period of anguish and suffering leading to a fulfillment in each other's arms. Most importantly, in spite of the often abstract, dream-like landscapes that formed the backdrops of the famous duets sung by Hemanta Mukhopadhayay and Sandhya Mukhopadhayay, the films were rooted in contemporary social reality. Thus, class, caste and race differences and problems of familial—or specifically, patriarchal—objections, were issues that the romantic couple had to address. Their desire and longing was moored in strong ethics and it is this that allowed them to go against the tide of tradition. Most of these films portrayed the middle-class, educated man migrating to the city from the village, and as a result, there were often detailed shots (mostly long shots) where one finds the hero wandering in the streets of the city. This wandering of the hero in the big city of Calcutta, though similar in incidence to Raj Kapoor's tramp wandering in the city of Bombay, has a completely different connotation and mood. Kapoor's tramp was modelled heavily on Charlie Chaplin and the communion in the end with the heroine (again mostly from the affluent class, like Suchitra's characters) was mostly passionately intimate. On the contrary, in positioning Uttam Kumar rarely in close-ups, most of the early directors of these films ensured that Uttam had the necessary identification of the battered Bengali who, like themselves, is a common man struggling to survive. Perhaps, Uttam's apparently mediocre features (as opposed to Barua's princely yet distant charm) helped in positioning him as one of the masses. This is important since in the '60s and the '70s, when Uttam's stardom became more self-assured and his stylizations more signature-driven, we could find more close-ups of Uttam in the typical sense where a 'star' is portrayed with all his famed mannerisms. There is another important aspect to the star-couple of Uttam and Suchitra. In line with the Victorian morality intact in the middle-class Bengali home, we find Uttam as the most ideal 'hero' Bengali cinema can dream of—modest and honest—a dependable 'star' who is the son, the father or the brother everyone hopes for, and of course the companion any girl looks for. As Smita Banerjee reflects:

> In films he is repeatedly shown as epitomizing the code of 'moral soundness' and 'integrity', a highly regarded middle class value, so much so that he is the trusted escort for unmarried girls on their journeys in *Suno Baro Nari* or the icon of morality and good behaviour in *Sagarika*. In *Saare Chuattor*, he is morally superior to all the other young men in the mess, and refuses to be a part of their youthful romantic pranks directed at Suchitra, while in *Agnipariksha* he is quite above the other young men surrounding Suchitra and displays moral courage and integrity in dealing with some ruffians who try to disrupt a party, while all the other men crouch in fear at the sight of the unruly crowd.[1]

---

[1] Smita Banerjee, 'Making of Uttam Kumar: The Star, the "True" Bhadralok', *Silhouette*, 3 September 2015, http://learningandcreativity. com/silhouette/uttam-kumar-the-star/, accessed on 15 May 2017.

These fairy-tale-like features defined the scope and the periphery of the film star, and that is why even in situations where he is debased, he never falls from grace. The hero doesn't have a despicable vice, and very importantly, in deference to Bengali middle-class virtues, his conjugation with the heroine (Suchitra in most cases) is almost asexual. The hero places mental and emotional virtues on such a high pedestal that it seems that physical attraction has to be subdued. This again is a significant departure from the pairs in Hindi cinema of the time, viz. Raj Kapoor and Nargis, where the physicality of their on-screen relation was never subdued and was, in almost all cases, exhibited triumphantly.

The '60s was an interesting decade as the star-couple partnered in only four films (and the same number the decade after). The major blockbuster undoubtedly was *Saptapadi* (1961) directed by Ajoy Kar. Uttam happened to be the producer of the film after his earlier collaboration with Kar in *Harano Sur* (1957), which also featured Suchitra Sen as his heroine. *Saptapadi* embodies the latent desire of the Bengali male of the early '60s—to win over a foreigner/anglo-Indian with pure Bengali charm and doggedness. Uttam Kumar as Krishnendu and Suchitra Sen as Rina Brown dazzled the silver screen with the inimitable and immortal song of the road 'Ei Path Jodi Na Sesh Hoy', which remains one of the most romantic Bengali film songs till date. It will forever be unknown as to why, after being such a success in the '50s, Suchitra and Uttam decided to drift apart, making only eight films in the next two decades— about a third of what they did in the '50s itself.

THE MAKING OF A MAHANAYAK

As an actor, Uttam Kumar kicked off a crescendo of great acting with Satyajit Ray's *Nayak* and a host of other films, including *Jhinder Bandi* and *Jatugriha* by another ace director, Tapan Sinha, and *Thana Theke Aschi*, *Chowringhee*, *Aparichito*, *Stree* and *Agniswar,* to name a few others. These films put him up on the podium not only as a star but also as one of India's finest actors of all time.

After the relative lack of success of *Kapurush-O-Mahapurush,* Satyajit Ray decided to make a film which would be commercial. He wrote the story himself, as with *Kanchenjungha,* modelling it on a matinee idol who is travelling to New Delhi to collect a prestigious award from the president. In a tribute to Uttam Kumar after his untimely death in 1980, Ray mentioned:

> I was not a film-maker yet when I first saw Uttam on the screen. I had heard of the emergence of a new hero and was curious to see what he was like... I saw three of Uttam's films in a row all made

by one of our ablest directors Nirmal Dey. First impression was certainly good. Uttam had good looks, a certain presence, an ease of manner and no trace of theatre in his performance... Uttam was certainly a star in the true Hollywood sense of the term. The question was: was he also an actor?... I was anxious to work with Uttam and wrote a part with him in mind.[2]

Ray continues:

I must say working with Uttam turned out to be one of the most pleasant experiences of my film-making career. I found out early on that he belonged to the breed of instinctive actors... I hardly recall any discussion with Uttam on a serious analytical level on the character he was playing. And yet he constantly surprised me and delighted me with unexpected little details of action and behavior which came from him and not from me, which were always in character and always enhanced a scene. They were so spontaneous that it seemed he produced these out of his sleeve.[3]

---

[2]*SUNDAY*, 3 August 1980, (IFSON: Special Ray Number, August 1992, pp. 34–35).
[3]ibid.

Ray here seems generous in praising the actor, who passed away a few weeks earlier—since later in a different interview to Andrew Robinson he was a bit scathing, perhaps quite unnecessarily:

> I never bothered to explain the character to him. So I never discovered whether he really understood the implications of the part. And it doesn't really matter whether he did or did not... I didn't discuss the psychology of the part at all. I merely told him that this is what you have to do. Trust me and it should be all right.[4]

This remark in particular creates a doubt in the critic's mind. This is perhaps the primary reason why Andrew Robinson himself failed to gauge the depth of Uttam's portrayal of Arindam, the hero:

> At root, Uttam Kumar doesn't project the real star quality that would make him so admired and disliked. He may well be the modern Krishna but where is his flute? He lacks élan and seems insufficiently masculine for a matinee idol; one looks in vain for a bit more Burton and a little less Bogart. With his penchant for self-pity and alcohol, Arindam seems to inherit something of

---

[4]Andrew Robinson, *Satyajit Ray: The Inner Eye*, Rupa and Co, 1990, p. 181.

the personality of Bengali screen heroes of an earlier period, whom Ray has always disliked. [5]

The western critic quite naturally wanted to measure Arindam's (and Uttam's) charisma against the benchmark of western heroes, who are necessarily more masculine physically. Any serious analysis of Uttam's earlier films will reveal his body language, which is firm yet complements that of the heroine—primarily Suchitra's. The two form a whole—the fulcrum of the modern family they had set out to explore and establish. Unlike Barua's pale fragility, Uttam's physique gave the Bengali male ego a sufficient boost to win a girl as coveted as Suchitra. The slight physical effeminacy that there is, is actually an extension of the mental coyness that makes him so endearing to women of any age or class. To measure him against a Burton or the later day macho heroes is to completely miss the social relevance comple that Uttam as a phenomenon stood to represent.

Ray repeated Uttam in his next film, *Chiriyakhana,* which is Ray's first detective film, based on Byomkesh Bakshi, the ace sleuth. In an interview with *Cineaste* magazine, Ray described *Chiriyakhana* as his most unsatisfying film:

---

[5]Ibid., pp. 180–81.

Chiriyakhana's a whodunit, and whodunits just don't make good films. I prefer the thriller form where you more or less know the villain from the beginning. The whodunit always has this ritual concluding scene where the detective goes into rigmarole of how everything happened, and how he found the clues which led him to the criminal. It's a form that doesn't interest me very much.[6]

Chiriyakhana remains a minor Ray film, yet it has two very important aspects. First, the nature of acting in Ray's films is almost always very low-key, less theatrical and realistic—something that is quite different from the acting prevalent in the popular space. Uttam Kumar preferred realistic acting, but he had to perhaps tone himself down for *Nayak*. In *Chiriyakhana,* Uttam picked up from where he had left off in *Nayak*. Though this occasionally meant that the sleuth had certain mannerisms which befitted a matinee-idol, in a larger context, it can be safely said that Uttam imbibed a style suitable for Ray films. Soumitra Chatterjee, for instance, finds this an excellent attribute of the actor. In a personal conversation, he once told me, 'The greatness of Uttam-da as an actor is revealed in

[6]Chiriyakhana, *Satyajit Ray Org*, http://www.satyajitray.org/films/chiriakhana.htm, accessed on 15 May 2017.

the way he picked up the Ray school of acting just by doing one film with Ray. I may have reservations with *Chiriyakhana* as a film but I don't find any flaw in Uttam-da's acting.' The second interesting aspect of *Chiriyakhana* is its influence on the psyche of the later Bengali film directors. There have been at least more than 5 Bengali films made in since 2010 directed by different directors and having different actors essaying the role of Byomkesh Bakshi. However, in all these occasions, one cannot ignore the physical resemblance that these Byomkeshes have with Uttam's portrayal of the sleuth. This is no coincidence and is indeed a ploy to make the character more endearing in a nostalgic way.

The moment of glory for Uttam Kumar came in 1968 when he received the Bharat Award for the Best Actor (renamed later as the Rajat Kamal Award for the Best Actor) in the National Film Awards, for his roles in *Chiriyakhana* (1967) and *Anthony Firingee* (1967). Uttam was active for thirteen more years after *Chiriyakhana*, his last Ray film. From the '70s, Uttam slowly turned more towards character roles, though his untimely death robbed us of our chance to witness his true potential as a matured character actor. Uttam's demise in 1980 created a void that remains mostly unfulfilled. The later heroes failed to match his charisma and his enormous capability of drawing the audience to the movie theatres.

His major compatriot was Soumitra Chatterjee, who had already ascended to a different plane right from the beginning due to his association with Ray and other stalwart directors of Bengali cinema, including Mrinal Sen and Tapan Sinha. Uttam's two terrific roles in the two Ray films made him acceptable to the cynical critics who had previously missed out on his immense acting prowess in their distaste for popular mainstream cinema. And it is always apt to refer to what Satyajit Ray had to say in his tribute to Uttam after the latter's death:

> I understand Utttam worked in something like 250 films. I have no doubt that well over 200 of them will pass into oblivion, if they have not already done so... An artist, however, must always be judged by his best work. On that basis and within the gamut in which his talent was best revealed, Uttam's work shows rare virtues of grace, spontaneity, and confidence. Such a combination is not easily come by, and it is hard to see anyone taking his place in the cinema of West Bengal in the near future.[7]

More than four decades later, Ray's prophetic prediction still holds true.

---

[7]*SUNDAY*, 3 August 1980 (IFSON : Special Ray Number, August 1992, pp. 34–35).

THE MOTHER ARCHETYPE

In 1895 (26th Chaitra, 1302 Bengali Calendar precisely), Rabindranath Tagore wrote the verse *Bangamata* (বঙ্গমাতা) which begins:

পূণ্যে পাপে দুঃখে সুখে পতনে উত্থানে
মানুষ হইতে দাও তোমার সন্তানে
হে স্নেহার্ত বঙ্গভূমি, তব গৃহক্রোড়ে
চিরশিশু করে আর রাখিয়ো না ধরে।

(Through good deeds and wrong, in sorrow and
happiness, downfall and uprise,
Allow your children to flourish and grow, to full
human potential realise.
Oh affectionate mother, in your lap most
comforting—
As children you must not keep them forever
nursing.)[1]

and then ends with the oft quoted:

শীর্ণ শান্ত সাধু তব পুত্রদের ধরে
দাও সবে গৃহছাড়া লক্ষ্মীছাড়া ক'রে।
সাত কোটি সন্তানেরে, হে মুগ্ধ জননী,
রেখেছ বাঙালী করে, মানুষ করনি।

---

[1]Animikh Rabindranath, 21 February 2012, https://animikha.wordpress. com/2012/02/21/%e0%a6%ac%e0%a6%99%e0%a7%8d%e0%a6%97% e0%a6%ae%e0%a6%be%e0%a6%a4%e0%a6%bebongomaatamother-bengal/, accessed on 22 November 2018.

(Grab your good-natured sons
and push them out there,
The world is theirs for the taking,
let them show no fear,
This great multitude of children,
Oh doting mother,
Confining them to a Bengali identity, you have not
let them discover the greater in humanity.)[2]

In the context of the Bengali psyche, Tagore's lines hold good to a large section of Bengalis even today, and helps one to understand the mother-child relationship in the Bengali household. Ray, in 1923, lost his father Sukumar Roy—a brilliant, uniquely creative person in his own right—at the tender age of two. It was Ray's mother, Suprabha, who took up the reins of the family and steadied them. Suprabha had a deep impact on Satyajit and his choices and decisions were, for quite some time, largely controlled and dictated by her. However, unlike the quintessential Bengali mother, Suprabha didn't cling on to Satyajit— it was due to his mother's persuasion that Ray went to Santiniketan to study fine arts in Vishva Bharati. In Ray's films however, the mother figure is not oft seen. Ray's cinema predominantly portrayed male characters

---

[2]ibid.

in important roles much more than female characters. Even in ones that are there, the mother archetype is difficult to locate.

However, the first two films of *The Apu Trilogy*—*Pather Panchali* and *Aparajito*—had Sarbajaya, Apu's mother, as the protagonist. In *Pather Panchali*, Sarbajaya is the wife of Harihar and the mother of Apu and Durga. The film was Ray's first, and apart from Harihar and Indir Thakrun, non-professional actors played most of the other characters. For Sarbajaya, Ray introduced Karuna Banerji, who happened to be the wife of Ray's friend Subrata Banerji. Karuna was a theatre actor and associated with IPTA (Indian People's Theatre Association) back then. She had impressive features that were in tune with the character profile of Sarbajaya in the novel on which the film was made. Some Bengali critics found her mannerisms slightly urban, which seems a bit harsh. For the western critic, there seems to be no aberration as Andrew Robinson comments:

As Sarbajaya, Karuna never felt any difficulty in identifying herself with a village housewife living in poverty. Although her life had been spent in cities (like Ray himself), she had been born in a large family in East Bengal and, like the Ray family of Sukumar's generation, she used to return to her ancestral village at festival time when she was growing up.[3]

Karuna gave a very solid performance in an ensemble cast where she didn't have much opportunity display portray her acting skills. The subtle change of emotion from affection towards her children, notably Apu, to her complete and cruel disregard of an ageing Indir Thakrun, was put forth commendably. In one of the most violent scenes in Ray's cinema, we find Sarbajaya dragging Durga by the hair and thrashing her black and blue when the neighbours allege that Durga has stolen their jewellery. In a contrasting scene, we find Sarbajaya bursting into tears as she confides the news of Durga's demise to Harihar.

Karuna Banerji, however, got her full in the second part of the trilogy—*Aparajito*. As Ray himself admitted:

The finest performance in *Aparajito*, a really inspiring and altogether a great one, was given by Karuna Banerji who was now a formidable actress. Especially moving were the scenes involving her and the grown up Apu, when she realizes that she is losing hold on her son. This made her last scenes particularly poignant because of

[3]Andrew Robinson, *The Apu Trilogy: Satyajit Ray and the Making of an Epic*, I. B. Tauris & Co Ltd, 2011, p. 49.

the absence of her son from her side. She had concealed the fact that she was ill when Apu had come home for his holidays, and taken her herbal medicine secretly.[4]

Aparajito remains one of the finest examples of world cinema where the delicate thread between a mother and her son has been exposed and explored. Sarbajaya wishes for Apu to stay back with her in their village home at the end of the film, but Apu has already tasted the opportunity that a city as romantic and resourceful as Calcutta can provide, and wishes otherwise. In *Aparajito,* unlike in *Pather Panchali,* we find Sarbajaya predominantly as the mother of Apu; her other roles as the wife of Harihar and the mother of Durga are either diminished or non-existent. This demanded that bonding in her acting and Karuna fulfilled it to perfection. As she recollects,

> I was absolutely overwhelmed by her personality. It all came so naturally to me. Every word, every look, every small movement, the deep attachment towards the alienated son, they all developed within me, as leaves grow outwards on the branch of a tree. Sounds poetic? But believe me, that is

---

[4]Satyajit Ray, *My years with Apu*, Penguin Books, 1996, pp. 113–14.

exactly how I felt whenever I had a chance to work with Manik. Not a single turn of the character that I portrayed was forced, illogical, artificial.[5]

Like her stoic and somber appearance on screen, she was, in real life as well, intelligent with a thoughtful mind. She was very outspoken too:

At that age, in general, I would speak my mind very openly without thinking much about whether it would hurt others or not. Sarbajaya did influence my personality quite a bit and that is why I am indebted to Satyajit Ray a lot. He was my husband's friend. I can recollect one incident during the shooting of *Aparajito*. On that day I was in a jovial mood with the crew since I didn't have much work. Suddenly Ray called me aside with a very grave face as if saying, 'How can Sarbajaya be so cheerful.' Actually, the schedule had been changed and I had to act out the scene where an ailing Sarbajaya would be sitting and waiting for Apu to return. So I needed to have teary eyes and a gloomy face to reflect the inner turmoil. Ray said, 'Bring tears to your eyes by looking at the sun.' I felt insulted—do I have to artificially strain myself so much to bring

---

[5]Andrew Robinson, *Satyajit Ray: The Inner Eye*, Rupa and Co, 1990, p. 98.

out the emotion? But then I had already become calm, so my reply stayed only in my mind.[6]

Sarbajaya in *Aparajito* specially remains a highlight of her career. It was liked and appreciated by the critics, and Andrew Robinson found it to be the best amongst all the characterizations in the three films that constitute the trilogy:

> If the remaining two-thirds of *Aparajito* is sometimes a less rich experience, notably in its Calcutta scenes, the viewer is compensated by the finest performance by any actor in *The Apu Trilogy*— not excluding Chunibala as Indir in *Pather Panchali* or Soumitra Chatterji as Apu in *The World of Apu*: that of Karuna Banerji as Sarbajaya. From her first appearance in a Benares courtyard to her death in the village of Mansapota at the end of *Aparajito*, she unifies it with her total conviction as Apu's mother—even more than with her performance in *Pather Panchali*.[7]

Karuna went on to be nominated in the Best Foreign Actress category in the 12th British Academy Film

---

[6]*Satyajit Ray: 70 Years Celebration*, Basumati Corporation Limited, 1992, pp. 14–15 (Translation author's).

[7]Andrew Robinson, *The Apu Trilogy: Satyajit Ray and the Making of an Epic*, I. B. Tauris & Co Ltd, 2011, p. 110.

Awards (popularly known as BAFTA) along with the likes of Ingrid Bergman, Giulietta Masina, Anna Magnani and Simone Signoret. Simone Signoret, who blazed a trail that year with her scintillating performance in Jack Clayton's *Room at the Top,* won the award.

Karuna acted in two more Ray films—as Harasundari, the sister-in-law of Doyamayee (played by Sharmila Tagore), in *Devi* and as Labanya, the wife of a domineering patriarch (a masterful Chhabi Biswas), in *Kanchenjungha.* Interestingly, in all the three characters in the four Ray films, Karuna played the mother figure. In *Devi*, she had a minor role and yet her jealousy and spite for Doyamoyee was effectively portrayed. The last appearance of Karuna in a Ray film, in *Kanchenjungha,* was interesting—'Being the wife of a most "undominating" husband in real life, it was really an entirely new experience to feel crushed yet rebellious under a dominating husband.'[8] Karuna delivered a nuanced performance to uphold the mood of such a submissive housewife. Yet in her moment of deliverance, she stood firm on her decision without succumbing to patriarchal pressures. Karuna didn't act much in Bengali cinema—her only notable other

---

[8]Andrew Robinson, *Satyajit Ray: The Inner Eye*, Rupa and Co, 1990, p. 138.

film being Mrinal Sen's polemical *Interview*. She was also roped in by the other genius of the Bengali triumvirate—Ritwik Ghatak—for his incomplete film *Kato Ajanare*.

Though Karuna Banerji as Sarbajaya provided the best performance in *Aparajito*, the mantle for the same in *Pather Panchali* arguably rests with Chunibala Devi as Indir Thakrun. Ray acknowledges: 'The most outstanding performance was of course Chunibala's. She came straight out of the pages of the novel, Indir Thakrun. She was thrilled to be back at work after thirty years of vegetable existence. She felt already at home in the part and never gave us a moment's trouble.'[9] Indir Thakrun represented the soul of rural Bengal at the time. She was impoverished and battered and yet had a zest for life. A childless widow, Indir Thakrun, quite ironically, was a different shade of the female archetype. She was immensely familiar as an ageing village woman with no one to look after her, and in her moments of brilliance, Indir Thakrun portrayed the pathos of a withering class.

However, finding Chunibala Devi for the role was a fascinating story in itself. Chunibala was primarily a stage actress in her days, but at the time of *Pather Panchali* she had already become quite old and fallen into

---

[9]Satyajit Ray, *My Years with Apu*, Penguin Books, 1996, p. 57.

real difficult times. Ray recollects his first interaction with her and his instant liking for the actress, the only one apart from Kanu Banerjee as Harihar who would previous cinema experience,

> She astounded us by singing a well-known lullaby. I had always thought it consisted of only six lines; she recited more than twenty! My thoughts were now racing. Why, she could sing too. Why not give old auntie an opportunity to sing? It would be most touching.
>
> 'Where will you be shooting?' asked Chunibala.
>
> 'Not in a studio, but in a cottage. You'll be playing the old cousin of a Brahmin priest...Do you think you can put up with the strain?'
>
> 'I think so, I have been conserving my energy for just this kind of opportunity...'[10]

Chunibala gave a scintillating performance, which fetched her the best actress award in the Manila Film Festival. A lot of praise goes to Ray for having the courage of casting such an old person for the role in his very first film (considering it took a long time to complete, stopped a number of times due to financial

---

[10]ibid., pp. 48, 49.

limitations). It was, like most actors and actresses in Ray's cinema, her finest acting exposition on screen and she added value to her performance by being extremely alert and helpful:

> From the beginning, Chunibala grasped Ray's intention that the film should display no artifice. 'She was constantly aware that authenticity was the touchstone of her performance,' he wrote. She was careful to wear her widow's sari with its torn portions knotted, as a poor woman in her position would do... Her memory for continuity was formidable. Ray recalled that she often picked up details he had missed, with comments like: 'That time it was my right hand which was wet', 'Wait, there was no sweat on my face before', 'In this shot my shawl wouldn't be covering me', 'Was my bundle in my right hand? No, it was in my left. My brass pot was in my right.'[11]

In 1961, commemorating the birth centenary of Bengal's greatest creative person, Rabindranath Tagore, Ray directed *Teen Kanya* (*Three Daughters*) adapting three distinct short stories of Tagore. The final part of the film, *Samapti* introduces Aparna Sen (nee Dasgupta),

---

[11]Andrew Robinson, *The Apu Trilogy: Satyajit Ray and the Making of an Epic*, I. B. Tauris & Co Ltd, 2011, pp. 51–52.

who went on to become a prominent heroine of Bengali cinema in the '60s and after, and then one of the most influential directors of India. In *Samapti,* Aparna plays Mrinmoyee, a tomboyish teenage girl who is married off against her wish to Amulya. We find Mrinmoyee's mother, failing to cope with her dilapidated condition, agreeing to marry Mrinmoyee off. In this process, she becomes abrasive and at times violent towards her daughter. However, the mother character which attracts attention is Amulya's mother. Like Sarbajaya in *Aparajito,* Jogmaya (played by an ebullient Sita Devi) in *Samapti* also wants her son to come back from the city to stay with her in their village home. She even tricks Amulya with a letter in which she fakes an illness to bring him back. The mother–son duo, though illuminated in a comic vein, mirrors the same relation in *Aparajito,* where an ailing Sarbajaya talks to Apu who is indifferent to his mother's attempted conversation and soon dozes off to sleep. Unlike Apu, Amulya is affluent and has an almost farcical association with so-called Western ideals and philosophy.

To understand the minimal existence of the mother character in Ray's cinema, it has to be understood that there is a significant correlation in the psychologies of Ray and Tagore. This semblance of their mental faculties is corroborated if one looks at Ray's poignant use of Tagore's stories as the subjects of his most resonant films. Interestingly, as many critics have pointed out, Tagore's women were, in most of cases, childless and ahead of their times. From Binodini to Charulata and Bimala to Mrinal, Tagore's protagonists are fiercely individualistic. They are strong, determined and dynamic, they are equal to men and at times superior to them where questions of morality and emotional pragmatism are concerned. On the contrary, Sarat Chandra Chattopadhyay's novels, that were undoubtedly more popular than Tagore's, had unvaryingly placed women at the feet of their men. The fates of Chattopadhyay's women are decided by the male protagonists, for whom their female counterparts are nothing more than subservient objects. In accordance with Tagore, some of Ray's important women characters from Charu to Karuna to Bimala have all been childless. Apart from *The Apu Trilogy* and a handful others, Ray, like Tagore, placed the women characters in his films in relation to their men as partners and not 'mother' figures.

In *Devi*,

> ...which is one of his most political films, Ray rails against the religious cowardice that forcibly commodifies a young daughter-in-law as the

'Goddess' incarnate based on an ambiguous dream. In a reverse mimesis, the relationship between the old zamindar (as the devoted 'son') and the 'Goddess' daughter-in-law (mentioned every time as the 'mother', though she is childless in reality) is grounded within religious overtones and has definite shades of incestuous desires.[12]

It is not difficult to correlate this to the decadence of the Bengali 'babu' in the social milieu of India since the middle of the last century, when the economic and political capital of India shifted permanently from Calcutta—to Bombay (which was already there in the map as the economic zone) and Delhi (the political capital of the idea of India since the days of the Muslim invaders), respectively. With this drift over the few decades, the Great Famine of early 1943 and the Partition of India in 1947, the veneer of the quintessential Bengali was cracked. However, many of them migrated to other cities, but that was more due to the surplus population after 1947. Even today, at the end of the day, the average Bengali wishes to remain in his own home in Bengal and within the confines

---

[12]https://www.news18.com/news/movies/most-interesting-mother-portrayals-in-bengali-cinema-1240221.html, accessed on 22 November 2018.

of its cultural and philosophical ambit, which make them aloof and cynical to others. This prudishness, on one hand, is attributed to the Bengali renaissance, which created such a flurry of moral, philosophical, literary and cultural virtues that generations of Bengali masticated on the same gleefully. On the other, and probably related, is this tendency of clinging to the roots even when the surroundings have withered in terms of opportunities. In the context of Bengali cinema, the depiction of the mother as the bearer and nurturer is what is expected and 'rational'.

There are no significant mother-daughter relations depicted in Ray's oeuvre the way we find them in Ritwik Ghatak's *Meghe Dhaaka Tara* or Rituparno Ghosh's *Unishe April*. Within this minimal representation, Ray's cinema has touched upon the latent tussle between the home and the world and the position of the mother in relation to her son; that too, in most of his early films. From the decade of the '60s until his final film *Agantuk* in 1992, the 'mother' didn't appear notably in Ray's cinema. He, like his cinema, travelled the world keeping love, reverence and respect for the mother and the motherland intact.

THE EXTRAORDINARY ORDINARINESS OF MADHABI MUKHERJEE

The early films of Satyajit Ray, with mostly classical subjects, predominantly had the male protagonists conveying the auteur's message on screen. Ray, throughout his career, has created unique character profiles. Even a number of cameo roles have profiles that are hard to forget. In creating these profiles, Ray generally relied on the overall physical attributes of the characters and never solely on the face. Hence, in Ray's films extreme close-ups are not seen that frequently, the way Ingmar Bergman holds the face of his lead characters or Michelangelo Antonioni frames the female face in his cinematic aesthetic. Ray's camera is predominantly static in that sense; it seldom attacks the character by moving forward, one notable exception being the close-up of Apu's face in *Apur Sansar* when Apu first comes to terms with the news of Aparna's death from her brother Murari.

After the first phase of films from 1955 until 1961 when he depended mostly on literary classics to form the backbone of his filmic narratives, Ray made *Kanchenjungha* in 1962 based on his own story set in the hill city of Darjeeling. However, Ray's first attempt to look at the contemporary urban life was with *Mahanagar* in 1963. In this directorial gaze, Ray also brought out, for almost the first time, a woman character who is confident in determining the course of her life even within the boundaries of a patriarchal society. Madhabi Mukherjee played Arati, the diminutive housewife of a middle-class Bengali home, who sets out to work in order to share the familial burden equally with her husband. Madhabi went on to act in two more Ray films, showing different shades of self-reliant womanhood. In all these films, she shares the same cinematic space as the male protagonists and in most cases, the camera focuses on her face far more than either of her male counterparts or the female characters of the previous Ray films. In these three films, the inner turmoil of the characters is best described always through Madhabi's facial expressions and her expressive eyes.

Madhabi Mukherjee started her film career in the '50s, but was first recognized as an actress of unparalleled depth in Mrinal Sen's 1960 film *Baishey Shraban* (*The Wedding Day*). Madhabi's low-key, subtle, subdued and yet tremendously poignant style (a style she uniquely shares with the other stalwart of Ray's cinema— Soumitra Chatterjee) resonated with the audience, and it is believed to have influenced Ray to think of casting Madhabi in *Mahanagar*. The Ray-Mukherjee association was brief and lasted only for three films, yet these three characters form the basis of women's identity in Ray's filmography. As Andrew Robinson mentions in his book *The Inner Eye*:

Madhabi Mukherjee, in *Mahanagar* all natural grace and intelligence, in *Charulata* is so finely tuned that we can enter her every thought and feeling. That, far more than her physical appearance, which can look quite ordinary, is what makes her profoundly beautiful. 'Is Charu the archetypal Ray woman?' someone once asked Ray. 'Yes, she is' he replied without qualification.[1]

In *Mahanagar*, the woman's journey from home to the outer world was strewn with confusion, self-doubt and at times guilt (for neglecting a young child at home). Madhabi's physical acting brought this out effectively, and yet beside her husband (played by Anil Chatterjee) she looked more assured and grounded. Madhabi had gone on record saying multiple times that she never felt like she was acting in *Mahanagar*, that she had known the character of Arati from within:

> When I first read the script of *Mahanagar*, I was stunned by its boldness. Here was a film-maker who talked about equality of sexes at a time when no one did. At the end of the film, when both the husband and wife lose their jobs, the husband consoles the wife, saying that at least one of us will

---

[1]Andrew Robinson, *Satyajit Ray: The Inner Eye*, Rupa and Co, 1990, pp. 161–62.

find a job in this metropolis. That's when they become equal citizens of the country.[2]

Chidananda Dasgupta, a close Ray associate and a renowned film critic, found Madhabi's acting flawless:

As the traditional middle-class housewife finding a new worth in herself, Madhabi Mukherjee is the perfect embodiment of the woman, torn between self-abnegation and self-respect. Even her looks are of the housewife lost in her chores who has, secretly in her somewhere, all the enticing mystery of woman. The enticing aspect is to unfold itself further in *Charulata*; but the possibility is indicated here, where Madhabi strikes the perfect note of hesitant emergence from behind the curtains of tradition.[3]

The third and last appearance of Madhabi in a Ray film was in *Kapurush* (*The Coward*) in 1965. Based on a short story, in this film, Madhabi as Karuna again embodies

---

[2]'I Don't Know What It Means To be an Ideal Satyajit Ray Heroine: Madhabi Mukherjee', *The Indian Express*, 31 August 2014, http://indianexpress.com/article/entertainment/regional/i-dont-know-what-it-means-to-be-an-ideal-satyajit-ray-heroine-madhabi-mukherjee/, accessed on 15 May 2017.
[3]Chidananda Dasgupta, *The Cinema of Satyajit Ray*, National Book Trust, India, 2003, p. 78.

a married woman with an identity which is distinct from the one she acquires due to her marriage. A tea planter's wife with a past, she meets her ex-lover who didn't have the courage to accept her choice, dignity and ability to take quick decisions for herself, and in turn for both their lives. As with Arati, here too Karuna is torn between her ideals, her own convictions, and the grind of reality. It will be interesting to note that for all the three characters played by Madhabi in Ray films, she has a latent power within her, a luminance which is rare and glaring, a strength of character which always puts her male counterparts to test—and not once could they match up to her. Satyajit Ray's assessment of women in the social construct is best evident in these films where, within the tropes of middle-class sentiment and psychology, he would position his female characters on a pedestal higher than that of men. These films reflect the choices women have in society and how the chances of them exercising the same make men uncomfortable, uncertain and weak.

The second Ray film in which Madhabi acted was *Charulata* (*The Lonely wife*) in 1964. Madhabi as Charu gave her best cinematic performance till date, one that is sublime and multilayered. *Charulata* is incidentally Ray's most acclaimed film as well, one he acknowledged as his most perfect. Ray had earlier made *Teen Kanya*

(1961) on three Tagore stories as a mark of respect, to commemorate the birth centenary of the legendry bard. However, the quintessential Tagore female character is one who is more mature and confident than most of her compatriots, and has an identity which is separate from her male partner. Hence, the character of Charu in Tagore's *Nasta-neerh* on which Ray based *Charulata* is a logical extension of Arati in terms of the aspirations of a woman with a sense of dignity and pride. Both Arati and Charu are rooted in the familial context and within the contours of their times, which actually make them human, with their frailties and more importantly their profound confusion about self and the changing identity that they are inevitably linked to. However, choosing Madhabi as a Tagore heroine was not easy. Most of Tagore's heroines are examples of supreme beauty and Madhabi's intelligent demeanour was not exactly suited to being one. There were other problems as well—the main being Madhabi's decaying teeth due to excessive eating of 'paan' (betel leaf). Ray was sure that he would manage to capture the glow in Madhabi's face, and yet his camera would be able to ignore the lower set of teeth. Throughout *Charulata,* one will notice that Ray had put the camera at a low angle looking up at Madhabi, so that even during the close-ups to depict the inner tension of Charu and her growing dilemma about her relation with Amal, the lower set of teeth are never to be seen!

According to Rabi Ghosh, who had acted with Madhabi in many films though never together in one of Ray's,

> Madhabi is basically an instinctive actress. In Ray she found a director who could explain to her everything about a character; and that not only amused Madhabi, it made her happy. And once an instinctive actress is happy, she's always tremendous. She knows her weapons, and how to throw them. That's why you get the inner feeling in her face in *Charulata*.[4]

This rapport between the actress and her director is the cornerstone of Madhabi's effortless performance, as she observes:

> Ray had an amazing ability to foresee his characters even before he made a film. He chose actors to fit those moulds. I guess I was a good fit for Charulata, so that was half the battle won. I did have to learn a few things that were in keeping with those times, like learning how to embroider.

---

[4]Andrew Robinson, *Satyajit Ray: The Inner Eye*, Rupa and Co, 1990, pp. 161–62.

Ray arranged for a teacher for that... My look was very simple and traditional. I wore the sari in the traditional way. I guess it was the way Ray and Subrata Mitra (cinematographer) captured me. I remember how Mitra had me put on this special pancake when I faced the camera. That's the only make-up I did... Bansi Chandragupta created a beautiful set for the sequence. Ray told me that the opera glass is a metaphor for the distance between Charulata and her husband. She uses the opera glass to bring things closer to her. While shooting the film, I didn't fully realise that it will be an incredible tableau where the camera follows Charulata around the house on what seems to be a typical afternoon in her life. While executing the sequence, I just internalised that concept.[5]

Ray changed the ending of Charulata from the original *Nasta-neerh*. He took a long time to finalize the ending and for Madhabi this wait to find out what happens to Charu heightened her confusion, which Ray skillfully used to his advantage to depict Charu's quandary.

[5]'I Don't Know What It Means To Be an Ideal Satyajit Ray Heroine: Madhabi Mukherjee', *The Indian Express*, 31 August 2014, http://indianexpress.com/article/entertainment/regional/i-dont-know-what-it-means-to-be-an-ideal-satyajit-ray-heroine-madhabi-mukherjee/, accessed on 15 May 2017.

Madhabi goes on to explain Satyajit Ray's unique style of handling his actors based on mutual respect and trust for the actor's abilities:

Mr Ray has an extraordinary feel for what is right in acting. He knows the exact point where the actor should stop, where he should hold back, where he should draw out the emotion a little more, where he should play upon several feelings quickly. It is this that makes every actor and actress, debutant and professional, young and old, give their best... In *Mahanagar*, my first Ray film, I found he was unique not because he used the lights and the camera differently, or went in for location shooting, or designed artistic sets... It was his ideas and thoughts, his conception of the total film, into which everything from actors to objects fitted in so perfectly as if they belonged there, which made him stand out from other directors. Take the lorgnette used by Charulata. The hunt for this quaint object through the Calcutta bazaars has been made much of as, indeed, Mr Ray's fastidious assembling of authentic objects in his sets to compliment the period and the mood of the story. It is not the lorgnette that was original but its use at that particular juncture, associated with that particular character and situation, which made the inanimate object underscore the loneliness and boredom of the young wife. The beauty lies in the contextual appropriateness. Throughout Ray's films you will see the tight network of motifs occurring again and again to heighten the tension like his background music.[6]

She continues,

I worked with Mr Ray in a very relaxed mood. From him I understood that playing a part well comes from feeling a character. Looking at his eyes I knew whether I had the right expression or not. He gave me the incentive to do my best and find myself in the part I played. His *Mahanagar*, *Charulata* and *Kapurush*, in which I had lead roles, scrutinize the conflicting relationships between man and woman in a changing middle-class society. Ray was very sensitive to the nascent desire for equality, self-reliance, self-expression and freedom in those women.[7]

Apart from the three films of Satyajit Ray, Madhabi

---

[6]Madhabi Mukherjee interview, 'The Genius of Satyajit Ray Issue', *Frontline* magazine, 20 December 1991, p. 88.
[7]ibid.

returned to Mrinal Sen's cinema in the latter's second part of the Calcutta Trilogy—*Calcutta 71*. She also acted as the central character in maverick director Ritwik Ghatak's unforgettable *Subarnarekha* (1965) in a completely different role and socio-psychological plane. Commenting on the differences between Satyajit Ray and Ritwik Ghatak in handling their actors, Madhabi observes:

> Satyajit-babu, if he was not satisfied with my take would usually say: 'Fine, but let's have another one.' He never attacks your self-confidence; he respects it. But Ritwik-da would start by saying: 'Look here. These are the words you have to speak. Will you be able to do it?—I rather doubt it.' Two things can then happen; either your confidence is totally shattered, or you lose your temper.[8]

In parallel to her breath-taking performances in the so-called 'art' films, Madhabi was also a formidable star in mainstream cinema being, occasionally paired with Uttam Kumar and Soumitra Chatterjee. It was Soumitra whom she could carve a niche on-screen chemistry with, which thrived on elite, middle-class sensitivities. Together they formed a representation

---

[8]Andrew Robinson, *Satyajit Ray: The Inner Eye*, Rupa and Co, 1990, p. 312.

of Tagorean classicism, which still continues to marvel the audience. Madhabi received her only National Film Award for Best Actress for *Dibaratrir Kabya* at the seventeenth National Film Awards in 1969 (it was then known as the Urvashi award).

What makes Madhabi such a formidable actress, and even more importantly, the main female face of Satyajit Ray's cinema? It is probably, as mentioned by Rabi Ghosh, her instinctive prowess at grasping the meat of the character. Ray's own clarity of thought about his profiles helped Madhabi flesh them out with such subdued effervescence. It is worth noting that in all the three films with Ray, the director exploited Madhabi's intense and expressive eyes—which are the seats of a range of emotions latent within the heart of the Bengali middle-class woman. Her craft has an effortless transition of expressions that shifts from one to the next without any disruption or glitch. Behind this seamless transformation lies a very sophisticated yet subtle technique in the way she manoeuvers her expression via her emotive eyes to light up a sequence and uses the same to portray her confusion, tension and agony. In personal exchanges with this author, Soumitra Chatterjee has often provided an analogy between a bird and an aeroplane while describing the depth of an actor:

...a good actor is like a bird. You can see it fly high, glide effortlessly and make swift plunges and alterations. However, you would never hear the mechanics behind the flight of a bird. It is that seamless. Whereas the flight of an aeroplane is always accompanied by heightened noise made by its different parts—you cannot afford to ignore the fact that the plane is actually flying. A bad actor, like an aeroplane will always make his or her craft visible to the audience to the point of being an eye sore. The power of an actor lies in concealing his craft and to remain sublimely quaint.

This analogy, which aptly defines the quality of Soumitra as an actor, also applies suitably to the acting of Madhabi Mukherjee. She entered the Bengali screen at a time when Suchitra Sen, whose star appeal was never in question, ruled it. There were others as well—Sabitri Chatterjee who was a stupendous actress, with an excellent streak of comic performances, as well as Supriya Chaudhuri who bloomed in a couple of Ritwik Ghatak's films and paired with Uttam Kumar to formidable success. For Madhabi, with her relatively ordinary looks, the task was cut out—she would never have the oomph of Suchitra or the backing that Supriya would receive being Uttam's live-in partner. She fulfilled her expectations by providing memorable profiles in the three Ray films that we discussed and a few others, which no other Bengali actress till date could emulate. Her total lack of self-consciousness probably helped her on screen and made her fit the role of the character she was playing. Mrinal Sen, whose *Baishey Shraban* actually launched Madhabi's career in the true sense, had described her quite aptly in a number of places—'She is extraordinarily ordinary.' There is probably no doubt that this extraordinary ordinariness helped Madhabi get under the skin of the characters she played with ease, poise and a rare dignity which glows bright even today.

SHARMILA TAGORE:
THE 'PRACHINA' AND 'NABINA' IN
RAY'S FILMS

In 1959 when *Apur Sansar*, the third part of *The Apu Trilogy*, was released, the audience found a new hero in Soumitra Chatterjee who, unlike the typical popular heroes of the silver screen, seemed real and grounded. Along with Chatterjee, there was another debut—that of Sharmila Tagore as Aparna, Apu's wife. Sharmila had a short screen presence in the film curtailed by Aparna's sudden death, but within the miniature reel time she had, she excelled as the young wife with a charming radiance. Ray, in the first two parts of the Trilogy as well, had introduced newcomers on screen in Karuna Banerji as Sarbajaya or the different Apu characters. However, with *Apur Sansar* Ray launched a duo that actually played the 'hero-heroine' and as history would have it, became two of the brightest actors in Indian cinema. In later films, Ray also launched the likes of Aparna Sen (then Dasgupta), Dhritiman Chatterjee or Dipankar De, to name a few. But, it all started with Soumitra and Sharmila in 1959.

However, finding a suitable Aparna for Apu was not easy. In *Aparajito*, the second part of *The Apu Trilogy*, Ray had to drop the character of Leela, Apu's teenage girlfriend, due to the want of a suitable actor. The omission of Leela was a significant loss in developing Apu according to many critics even today. While making the third and final part, Ray was cautious about finding the appropriate Aparna right from the beginning. Legend has it that Ray advertised in the newspapers asking for photographs of young teenage girls to play Apu's wife. There were more than a thousand aspirants, but none of the photographs seemed fine to Ray. Eventually, his crew apparently found Sharmila in a dance recital. The hunt extended to her school and it was then discovered that she had a Tagore lineage, though she wasn't a direct descendent of Rabindranath. More importantly, Sharmila's younger sister Tinku had already acted in Tapan Sinha's award winning film *Kabuliwala,* which became internationally famous once it claimed attention in the Berlin Film Festival. These coincidences somehow convinced Ray that getting permission from her parents would probably not be exceedingly difficult. On the day when Sharmila visited Ray's home for the first time, Ray could immediately sense that he had found his Aparna though a frock-clad early teen Sharmila seemed distant from the character. She was immediately changed into a sari by Bijoya, Ray's wife, her hair knotted into a bun, and it seemed a miracle had happened!

The first day of shooting for Sharmila was the scene where Apu brings his young bride Aparna to his single-room flat in Calcutta that faces the railway tracks. Sharmila remembers,

Soumitra and I were standing outside the closed door on the set and the camera was the other side. Ray called out, 'Camera, Action'. Soumitra asked me if I was feeling nervous. I said, 'No, I am not feeling nervous at all'. So, he opens the door, looks back at me and says, 'come in', I cross the threshold and enter the room and look around for a couple of minutes more and sigh and there are a couple of extra shots and I sometimes wonder whether he kept that particular scene on purpose because Aparna, the character—and I—had no idea what lay across the other side, nor did Aparna, she had no idea when the door opened what was there.[1]

Sharmila recollects her experiences in first film with Ray:

I had no lines to say on that (first) day. But on the second day, Manik-da asked me to speak a long dialogue. Seeing I found it difficult to say the dialogue, he broke it into short pieces... Manik-da did not give me too many instructions. He allowed me to do what came to me naturally. Only now

---

[1]Sharmila Tagore, 'How Satyajit Ray Changed My Life', *Asian Culture Value*, http://asianculturevulture.com/portfolios/sharmila-tagore-how-satyajit-ray-changed-my-life/, accessed on 15 May 2017.

and then he would come right up to me and say very softly, 'Rinku (Sharmila's pet name), just try it like this' and showed me... He used to chew his handkerchief, so much so that he needed a new handkerchief every day. I found him chewing his handkerchief whenever he was sitting alone next to the camera, deep in thought... I also remember that he ate fried fish and mistidoi every afternoon. One other thing I remember is that he frequently whistled different tunes and he whistled them beautifully. Many years later, immediately after he had received the Oscar for lifetime achievement, I interviewed him on behalf of a TV channel. I asked him whether he had kept up his habit of whistling. He moved his head indicating he had not.[2]

Aparna's screentime in *Apur Sansar* was close to thirty minutes, which forms about a quarter of the film. However, even within that short span, Ray created an environment of romantic lyricism ably supported by his actors Chatterjee and Tagore. The intimate details of their domestic life are simple and sweet: this paves

[2]Arup K De, 'Satyajit Roy's Sharmila Tagore', *The Statesman*, 13 September 2015, http://www.thestatesman.com/news/supplements/satyajit-roy-s-sharmila-tagore/89695.html#kv8T9T6d6RXDia3r.99, accessed on 15 May 2017.

way for the profundity of Apu's sense of loss due to Aparna's untimely death during the birth of their son Kajal. Apu's innocence is amplified by Aparna's naivety; Apu's confusion and hesitation smothered by Aparna's direct simplicity. Sharmila Tagore put forth a very engaging performance in the limited opportunity she had. Her performance was lauded immensely at home in Bengal as well as outside. Marie Seton, for example, found Sharmila had 'endowed the girl not only with loveliness but, as the next sequences reveal, a great deal of character.'[3]

However, she had to pay one price for that: 'I was told that if I decided to act in a film, I would have to leave school. The principal of my Bengali-medium school felt that having a filmstar amongst her students would be scandalous.'[4] Sharmila's father tried to reason with the principal, but that didn't yield results and Sharmila had to be transferred to a different school away from Calcutta after *Apur Sansar* was made.

This shift of school and city actually helped Sharmila broaden her horizons and she was back in Ray's very next

---

[3]Marie Seton, *Portrait of a Director*, Penguin Books India, 2002, p. 110.

[4]Arup K De, 'Satyajit Roy's Sharmila Tagore', *The Statesman*, 13 September 2015, http://www.thestatesman.com/news/supplements/satyajit-roy-s-sharmila-tagore/89695.html#kv8T9T6d6RXDia3r.99, accessed on 15 May 2017.

film, *Devi,* pairing up again with Soumitra Chatterjee as Doyamoyee and Umaprasad, respectively. Unlike *Apur Sansar,* in *Devi,* Sharmila Tagore was at the heart of the film playing the titular 'devi' (goddess). For veteran film critic and Ray's long-time friend Chidananda Dasgupta the choice of Sharmila to play Doyamoyee was not without reason: 'It was not for nothing that Sharmila was cast as the goddess in *Devi;* she is distinctly the type described in Bengal as Durga-like. Her similarity to the image of goddess, at the beginning and end of the film, is very marked.'[5]

In a cruel series of consequences triggered by Doyamoyee's father-in-law Kalikinkar's (Chhabi Biswas) dream of Doyamoyee being the incarnation of Goddess Kali, we find how Doyamoyee is sucked into rituals and unscientific expositions of customs and expectations. The film is Ray's first look at the dichotomy between tradition and modernity, based on religious practices. Sharmila's Doyamoyee was a perfect demonstration of a timid, young, rural yet affluent Bengali housewife of the late nineteenth century whose shift of emotions from the initial coyness with her husband to her disbelief at being hailed as a goddess and finally her insanity at the end which leads to her probable demise is commendable

---

[5]Chidananda Dasgupta, *The Cinema of Satyajit Ray*, National Book Trust, India, 2003, p. 149.

and extraordinary. The film, like *Apur Sansar,* starts with lovely domestic moments between Doyamoyee and Umaprasad before the latter sets off for Calcutta to continue his studies. In a role reversal of sorts from *Apur Sansar,* here we find Sharmila hogging most of the screen time rather than Soumitra, who comes in bits and pieces mostly as a liberal and Western-educated young man, in a confrontation with his father's blind religious beliefs that rocks the family. In those initial moments, we also find lovely snippets of togetherness between Doyamoyee and Kalikinkar when Doyamoyee is seen to apply oil on her father-in-law's feet as part of the age-old Hindu practice of serving the elderly. To a few Western critics this action is suggestive of the unconscious sexual tension that Kalikinkar experiences for Doyamoyee, and which he subjugates by turning her into the incarnation of Kali. In the dialogue between the two that is driven mostly by Kalikinkar, he tries to gauge some minute intimate details between Doyamoyee and Umaprasad. That there will be a storm to set apart the lives of these characters is seeded mostly in that sequence.

Among all the five characters that Sharmila has played in Ray's films, Doyamoyee is probably the most difficult one. Considering the fact that the actress was still a teenager at that time makes the performance even more commendable. According to her,

> The exploitation of Dayamoyee in the name
> of religion made a profound impression
> on my mind... I was weighed down as if by an
> inexplicable burden during the shooting. The
> dark ambience created by Bansi-da (Bansi
> Chandragupta), the smell of the burning incense
> sticks, the garlands around my neck and all the
> rest of it made me feel listless and depressed. I felt
> isolated because no one spoke to me during the
> breaks, which added to the feeling of oppression.
> But it was probably just that which helped my
> performance. Everyone around me appreciated
> the way I played the part of Doyamoyee.[6]

Andrew Robinson analyses Sharmila's performance and
finds it to be a sensitive portrayal:

> Doya throughout is only half-perceived; although
> she is very sensitive and alert, we can only guess at
> the true thoughts behind her sloe-like eyes—she
> seems composed mainly of instinct. According to
> the teenage Sharmila Tagore speaking a few years

---

[6]Arup K. De, 'Satyajit Roy's Sharmila Tagore', *The Statesman*, 13 September 2015, http://www.thestatesman.com/news/supplements/satyajit-roy-s-sharmila-tagore/89695.html#kv8T9T6d6RXDia3r.99, accessed on 15 May 2017

afterwards, 'Devi was what a genius got out of me, not something I did myself.' Ray gives her more credit than that. He didn't direct her nearly to the same extent as in *The World of Apu*. 'She once said to me, "But Manik-da, you're not directing me so much." I had to tell her I felt she was doing it all right. "Why should I direct you when you don't require any direction of that kind?"'[7]

With the success of her first two films, Tagore became an actress whom people were curious about and eager to see. She continued to make her mark in films like *Sesh Anka* (her first with Uttam Kumar), *Nirjan Saikate* (her first in a Tapan Sinha film), *Chhaya Surjo* (another complex character which she essayed with finesse) and *Kinu Goyalar Gali* (pairing again with Soumitra Chatterjee in a complex urban drama). In 1964, Sharmila migrated to Bombay and made her first Hindi film opposite Shammi Kapoor in *Kashmir Ki Kali*. There was no looking back for Tagore as she continued to triumph with her skills and star quotient in commercial Hindi cinema. Throughout the late '60s till the mid-'70s Sharmila remained one of the top heroines of Hindi cinema. She teamed up with Rajesh Khanna and the duo provided seven all-time box office hits in *Aradhana, Safar, Amar Prem,*

---

[7]Andrew Robinson, *Satyajit Ray: The Inner Eye*, Rupa and Co, 1990, p. 124.

Chhoti Bahu, Daag, Raja Rani and *Avishkaar*. She also starred in Gulzar's 1975 film, *Mausam,* in a double role and bagged her first National Film Award for Best Actress. She returned to the National Film Awards later in 2003 to claim the award for the Best Supporting Actress for her role in *Abar Aranye,* which happened to be a sequel to Ray's *Aranyer Din Ratri.*

Amongst all the actors and actresses who migrated from Bengali cinema to the Hindi film industry, Sharmila Tagore has no match, not even Mithun Chakraborty, who was the lone other Bengali star of Hindi cinema (Jaya Bhaduri and Rakhee were excellent actresses, but couldn't quite qualify as superstars of Hindi cinema the way Tagore and Chakraborty did)[8]. Sharmila was very clear with her conscience as to why she moved to Hindi cinema, considering not only her conservative family background, but also a prudish Bengali psyche in general which in the '60s castigated Hindi cinema as cheap and of low class. She clarifies,

> I went to Mumbai because I wanted to be economically independent. Actors and actresses were poorly paid in Kolkata. I am happy that I

---

[8]Mithun's first film *Mrigaya* was in Hindi, directed by Mrinal Sen; he did his acting training in FTII, Pune (he had his Hindi brush up early on that way), and he started to try out his luck in Bollywood in his very second film, *Do Anjane.*

went to Mumbai... However, I never hesitated to get back whenever I was offered a suitable role in a Bengali film. Shakti-da (Shakti Samanta) gave me a break by giving me the female lead in *Kashmir Ki Kali*. He was not pleased when I gave Manik-da dates for *Aranyer Din Ratri*. I was then in the middle of working for *Aradhana*. I also rushed to Kolkata when Manik-da invited me to work in *Seemabaddha*, though my schedule was pretty hectic those days in Mumbai.[9]

Before *Aranyer Din Ratri* was made in 1970, Sharmila returned to Ray's oeuvre in *Nayak* in 1966. For Sharmila, *Nayak* was important in two aspects. Firstly, it was her second film with Uttam Kumar, the superstar, and she had by then already tasted success with Hindi matinee idols. Secondly, after *Devi,* there was a gap before she returned to work with Ray in *Nayak*. By that time, working with other directors in Calcutta and Bombay (erstwhile Mumbai) helped her grow as an actress. Aditi in *Nayak* marks Sharmila's transition from the coy, naïve domestic Bengali girl of her initial films to a sophisticated Indian woman in the later

---

[9]Arup K. De, 'Satyajit Roy's Sharmila Tagore', *The Statesman*, 13 September 2015, http://www.thestatesman.com/news/supplements/satyajit-roy-s-sharmila-tagore/89695.html#kv8T9T6d6RXDia3r.99, accessed on 15 May 2017.

Hindi ones. Even in her last two appearances in Ray's films, the difference in sophistication is markedly pronounced. One may recall a scene in Ray's *Charulata* where Charu and Amal engage in wordplay, with the literal opposites 'prachina-vs-nabina' referring to the dichotomy between the naïve/traditional and the modern woman. Sharmila is one actress (along with Madhabi) who successfully performed these opposite roles in different character in Ray's work. *Nayak*'s primary characters is predominantly based on Uttam Kumar's acting abilities; the importance and scope for Sharmila were minimal. Her natural smartness that she had developed by then introduced the necessary amount of svelte polish required of the character, who is supposed to be relatively unperturbed by the charisma of the matinee idol whom she dares to interview. Sharmila recollects working with Uttam,

I had worked with him in *Sesh Anka*, a Bengali film made in 1963... Manik-da asked me to wear glasses in *Nayak* because he wanted me to look older than my age. Uttambabu gave an excellent performance in the film. Despite being a superstar, he was always very courteous and humble on the sets.[10]

---

[10]ibid.

Sharmila's last stint with Ray was in the second part of the 'Calcutta Trilogy' named *Seemabaddha* in 1971. Like in *Nayak* or even *Aranyer Din Ratri*, Sharmila in *Seemabaddha* plays role of the 'conscience'. Tutul (Sharmila) is almost like a moral barometer against whom the protagonist's virtues and vices are judged and valued. Interestingly again, like in *Charulata*, Tutul, Shyamalendu and Dolon (Shyamalendu's wife and Tutul's elder sister) form the proverbial triangle with a very subtle undercurrent of sexual tension. However, while in *Charulata,* Amal and Charu shared a love that rocks the nest, in *Seemabaddha,* even though Shyamalendu finds himself more akin to Tutul than to Dolan, there is no explicit love interest between the two. In the penultimate scene, on the day that Dolon is celebrating the Shyamalendu's promotion (he is visibly happy as well), we find Tutul and Shyamalendu sitting face to face in their plush living room and Tutul slowly taking off the wrist-watch that Shyamalendu had given her earlier, during her stay at their place. It symbolically ends their relation which, to an extent, was platonic despite the undertone of tension.

Sharmila Tagore appeared as Aparna in *Aranyer Din Ratri* in 1969—her fourth appearance in a Ray film before her last as Tutul in *Seemabaddha*. Aparna in *Aranyer Din Ratri* was no doubt the most complex character of the five that Sharmila had to portray, as well as her third pairing with Soumitra Chatterjee (who played Ashim who was quite an alter ego of Apu). The shooting location was entirely outdoors at the Betla forests, now in Jharkhand (then Bihar). She recollects:

> We did shooting for around two to three hours early in the morning and then again, latish in the afternoon. It was so hot that it was humanly impossible to work in between. Samit (Bhanja), Subhendu (Chatterjee), Rabi-da and I stayed together in one dak-bungalow. It was continuous adda. Rabi-da made us laugh so much. Manik-da and Soumitra (Chatterjee) stayed in one dak-bungalow and Kaberi-di (Bose) and Simi (Garewal) in another. In the evening, we would often visit tribal villages, interact with the inhabitants and also dance with them. It was great fun. I enjoyed every moment of it.[11]

The film was a scathing comment on the petty bourgeoisie of the urban cities. Criticized primarily by the Bengal press at the time of its release for being escapist and aloof to the political situation of the times (during the heightened Naxalite movement in Calcutta

---

[11]ibid.

and Eastern India) the film ironically got rave reviews from their international counterparts who found enough lyrical allegory in the film to stand the test of time. After nearly half a century since its release, the film is still relevant and resonates even more, considering the dissociation of the urban class with the common Indian as depicted in the film. Like the other two films of her second phase, in this one, too, Sharmila plays the 'conscience' character. Her presence is less vocal here than that of Aditi in *Nayak* but not as muted as Tutul in *Seemabaddha*. She is the balance between Ashim's crude, urban and distasteful arrogance (a class she belongs to as well) and the naïve, rural Chowkidar—she is the bridge between insanity and humanity, the only hope for Ashim to return as a man of moral courage as the film ends. This is primarily the reason why Aparna is complex—her pathos and sensitivities and her social, economic and political standing are what make the character almost unreal within the realm of its existence. The role and Sharmila's characterization, however, don't appeal Andrew Robinson who comments:

> The problem lies not with the screenplay but with Sharmila Tagore's portrayal of Aparna: her one-upmanship, her fashionable hairdo and clothes and her manner of speaking, which

owes something to Bombay-coy, just are not psychologically consistent with a girl who nurses these twin sources of grief. In a film less finely tuned than *Days and Nights in the Forest*, this would hardly interfere, but it is definitely a weakness by Ray's standards, particularly as he regards Aparna as the character 'you are supposed to sympathise with.' ...in Aparna unlike Charu (or Aditi of *Nayak*, for that matter), Ray goes a little too far; as well as appearing sensitive and mature, Aparna seems slightly supercilious and vain about her superiority.[12]

Sharmila continued to reign supreme in the Bollywood film industry for quite some time in the early '70s, but would never return to a Ray film after *Seemabaddha*. There were a few other times when Sharmila's name was in contention but she somehow missed doing the roles:

Manik-da also wanted me to play Charu in *Charulata*. He even gave me the script, but later changed his mind. The same happened in *Ashani Sanket*. I was his first choice but then it became an Indo-Bangla production and Babita played Ananga. I also wanted to play Bimala in *Ghare Baire*

---

[12]Andrew Robinson, *Satyajit Ray: The Inner Eye*, Rupa and Co, 1990, p. 199.

but Swatilekha proved more fortunate than I.[13]

These dejections notwithstanding, Sharmila is the actress who acted in the most number of Ray films as the heroine and among all the performers in the cinema of Satyajit Ray who played central characters, she is second only to her co-debutant in *Apur Sansar*, Soumitra Chatterjee. Sharmila, like many of the actors and actresses 'discovered' by Ray, acknowledged the legacy of the towering personality through a rich tribute to the master in one of her own writings:

> Satyajit Ray with his rich legacy meant many things to many people. For me, he was Manik-da who gave me a new life. I owe him a huge personal debt. He taught me how to look at cinema, how to be in front of the camera, how to think in character, how to enjoy a language and he taught me the importance of the 'moment'. He led by example and from him I learnt the value of commitment to one's work. Fifty-seven years ago, a girl of 13 as the young bride Aparna on that first day's shooting at the technician's studio, took

---

[13]Arup K De, 'Satyajit Roy's Sharmila Tagore', *The Statesman*, 13 September 2015, http://www.thestatesman.com/news/supplements/satyajit-roy-s-sharmila-tagore/89695.html#kv8T9T6d6RXDia3r.99, accessed on 15 May 2017

her first tentative steps across the threshold to a mysterious unknown. Her life changed forever as she entered the enchanting, magical world of cinema, which has given and continues to give her so much.[14]

---

[14]Sharmila Tagore, 'What Satyajit Ray Left Us is an Inheritance of Endless Possibilities', *The Wire*, 11 September 2015, http://thewire.in/10476/what-satyajit-ray-left-us-is-an-inheritance-of-endless-possibilities/, accessed on 15 May 2017

THE CHILDREN'S WORLD OF
SATYAJIT RAY

In world cinema, the term 'children's films' is primarily used for films with child characters, where the narrative evolves through their perspectives. Needless to say, this premise alone can't be used to classify any film as a children's film. From *Ivan's Childhood* to *400 Blows*, from *Bicycle Thieves* to our own *Pather Panchali,* there are numerous examples in world cinema where children play very important roles and yet these films are never 'children's films' by any definition. Similarly, quite a few of Charlie Chaplin's masterpieces have been equally devoured by adults and children. Indian cinema in general and Bengali cinema in particular have a dearth of children's films. However, of the few who would lead that short list, the name of Satyajit Ray would feature at the top. Ray started writing stories for children and adolescents in the late '60s to boost the revival of the family magazine *Sandesh*. Since then, till his death, there was no looking back for Ray as a writer for young minds. His iconic detective character Feluda or Professor Shonku, the scientist, along with dozens of other short stories, have made him a best-selling author even now, more than two decades after his demise.

THE CHILD HEROES

Ray's first two films, which are part of *The Apu Trilogy,* revolve around the character of Apu, a dreamy-eyed rural Bengali boy. In *Pather Panchali,* Ray had to put in quite an effort to get the Apu he was looking for. Apu's teenage sister, Durga, was the other child character in the film. Uma Sen (nee Dasgupta), who played Durga, reminisced about Subir Banerjee, who played the young Apu:

> Subir was so young that he had to be literally cajoled into acting, with inducements and by explaining everything that he needed to do. Yet the innocence of his face, the way it conveys feelings and emotions, through frequent blinking of his eyes, created such an enthralling portrait, thanks to Satyajit Ray's magic wand.[1]

Talking about the sequence of Indir Thakrun's death Uma remembers,

> Manik-da instructed me on how to convey an expression of bewilderment at the shock mingled with helplessness. He was happy with

---

[1]Uma Sen, 'We Still Hum the Song of the Little Road...', *The Pather Panchali Sketchbook*, Harper Collins India, 2016, p. 94.

my performance. But I just couldn't do the next scene—Durga silently weeping at Indir Thakrun's verandah. But genius that he was, Manik-da managed to overcome this shortcoming on the part of the actor by capturing Durga's tearful eyes in chiaroscuro, creating a mournful ambience. Manik-da worked on my performance sequence by sequence, one at a time. Take, for example, the scene of the theft of Tuni's garland of beads. A humiliated Sarbajaya is beating Durga mercilessly. Manik-da advised Karuna-di not to think of my getting injured but to go on beating me, pulling me by the hair and throwing me out. Everyone remembers Karuna-di's extraordinary performance in that scene as, driven by anger and humiliation, she loses all sense of proportion.[2]

Uma recollects the unique way Ray had of bringing out the characters in the children. He 'never gave instructions to the children in the presence of others. It was always whispered exclusively to each child so that what he wanted us to do was like a secret between just the two of us. We liked him so much that we wanted to please him.'[3] Uma

---

[2]Uma Sen interview, 'The genius of Satyajit Ray Issue', *Frontline* magazine, 20 December 1991, p. 88.
[3]ibid., p. 95.

gave a scintillating performance as Durga, and so did Subir as Apu, though it was difficult to get Subir to act. Even today, Subir recollects how much fun it was at the location and the shooting days were like a picnic to him. There was no fear or anxiety. He also takes pride in his association with Apu, who became an iconic character in Indian cinema:

> Kaka-babu had said, 'Why are you hesitant to allow your son to act in a film? It's taken me so long to find my Apu. I have seen over two hundred boys, but couldn't find anyone suitable. The film won't be possible without him.' Then he said something that my parents couldn't disregard. He said, 'I'll make a film that will alter the course of Bengali film-making. Today no one knows your son or me. But a day will come when the whole world will know us.' Imagine the self-confidence and far-sightedness a director must have to say something like this even before starting work on his first film.[4]

In *Aparajito*, the second part of *The Apu Trilogy*, Pinaki Sengupta (as the young Apu) and Smaran Ghoshal (as the adolescent Apu) played the role of Apu jointly.

---

[4]Subir Banerjee, 'Still Apu After All These Years', *The Pather Panchali Sketchbook*, Harper Collins India, 2016, p. 99.

Pinaki reappeared in Ray's fourth film *Jalsaghar* as the son of the zamindar played by Chhabi Biswas.

Two of India's most important actors—Sharmila Tagore and Aparna Sen—debuted in Ray films, the former in *Apur Sansar* and the latter in *Samapti* (the third story of the triplet *Teen Kanya*). Both of them were in their early teens in these films, though none of the characters were children in the strict sense of the term. In *Postmaster*, the first story of *Teen Kanya*, Chandana Banerjee plays Ratan. She steals the show with her heart wrenching performance as a young innocent servant of a postmaster who treats her with respect (unlike her other masters) and then finally returns to the city, leaving Ratan absolutely shattered. Chandana was such a powerful actress that she got effusive admiration from a seasoned actor like Anil Chatterjee (who played the role of the postmaster).

Andrew Robinson goes to the extent of branding Chandana as the 'discovery' of the film. He argues, 'Her miraculously natural acting, combined with "the squirrel-like character of her face", in Seton's phrase, defines her vividly as an individual; and yet she can also seem to represent all the world's struggling children.'[5] Robinson quotes Ray, who was equally in praise of

---

[5]Andrew Robinson, *Satyajit Ray: The Inner Eye*, Rupa and Co, 1990, p. 130.

Banerjee: 'She turned out as a fantastic actress: ready, no tension at all, and intelligent and observant and obedient—perfect to work with. Anil (Chatterjee), who played the postmaster, was constantly worried that no one would look at his performance with her there on the screen.'[6]

Ray, who was never a propagandist of his social or political beliefs, made a short film in 1964 called *Two*. It had only two child characters—two boys, an affluent one who staying in his house of toys (though he seems lonely since no one is ever found in the house) and the other poor, staying in a slum that the rich boy can see from his window. Their non-verbal interaction, the struggle between the rich and the poor in society is what Ray aims to portray in an oversimplified script of fifteen minutes. The loneliness of the urban-rich child is repeated again in Ray's later short film *Pikoo* (1980), where Pikoo is a young boy through whose eyes we see changing interpersonal relationships among the adults and also the evolution of his relationship with nature.

CHILDREN AS PASSIVE SUBJECTS

In the last part of the Apu trilogy, *Apur Sansar*, Apu is shown as a grown up adult. In the third act of the film,

---

[6]ibid.

the audience is introduced to Kajal, Apu's son, who is growing up on his own at his maternal household, oblivious to Apu. Alok Chakravarti, who played Kajal, happened to be a relation of Soumitra Chatterjee who played Apu in the film. Although quite reminiscent of Apu in *Pather Panchali*, unlike Apu's sublime temperament, Kajal is feisty, as life would have taught him to be. Yet, his poignant eyes and his mistrust for his biological father remain as one of the most brilliant portrayals, devoid of crass sentimentalism and cheap melodrama. Though short, the interaction between Apu and Kajal in *Apur Sansar* unquestionably reminds the audience of another noble film—*Bicycle Thieves* by Vittorio De Sica.

In *Kanchenjungha*, too, the young daughter of Anima and Sankar plays a vital role in mending the differences between her parents and saving their marriage, though she has a passive presence in the entire narrative of the film. Likewise, children in some of the other Ray films serve the role of defining the other more active characters, or in shaping the structure of the narrative. For example, in *Devi*, the young nephew is the mirror against whom Doyamoyee's supposed incarnation as the goddess is administered; in *Mahanagar,* the son is the point of dilemma for the middle-class Bengali woman of the '60s; in *Aranyer Din Ratri*, the young son provides the necessary alter-tension to the repressed sexual edge of the widow Jaya. Even in the Tagore stories—*Charulata* and *Ghare Baire*—it is the lack of a child which, to an extent, defines the lead female characters and explains the choices they make in deliberating their actions. In the last two films—*Shakha Proshakha* and *Agantuk*—as well, young children have definitive objectives. In *Shakha Proshakha*, the grandson is the one from whom the old industrialist learns about the corruption his sons indulge in, which leaves him shattered and shocked. In *Agantuk*, the docile child is the only person who, from the very beginning, believes in the stranger—he is, to Ray, the only hope for humanity and the only chance to combat the adult world riddled with distrust, anarchy and discord.

CHILDREN'S FILMS

As mentioned above, Indian cinema in general has seldom ventured into the genre of 'children's films' even though time and again film-makers have confessed that this is a relatively safe genre, where results at box office are slightly more predictable than the so-called mainstream romance/drama films. Particularly for Bengali cinema, it is rather sad, since Bengali literature has a rich heritage of works for children. Amongst the front-runners in cinema apart from Ray, Ritwik Ghatak made *Bari Theke Paliye* for young minds and Tapan Sinha made a few, including *Sabuj Dwiper Raja*, *Safed Haathi* and *Aaj Ka Robin Hood*.

Ray's first venture into children's films was with the 1968 masterpiece *Goopy Gyne Bagha Byne (GGBB)*. Fresh from the failure of *Chiriyakhana*, a film Ray had always wanted to forget, and the lukewarm box office response of the two earlier films *Kapurush-o-Mahapurush* and *Nayak*, *GGBB* was a welcome break and a meaningful deviation in his career. Andrew Robinson further adds that it was probably the first time Ray wanted to make a film that would appeal to his son Sandip as an intrinsic children's film, and had a desire 'to reach out to children by giving them something vital, original and Bengali, which he felt did not necessarily mean having a child actor.'[7] *GGBB* was based on Ray's grandfather Upendrakishore's popular story of the same name. Though the grandeur of the narrative demanded it be shot in a coloured film, unfortunately, due to budget constraints, Ray had to settle for black-and-white film stock for *GGBB*. Considering the elaborate outdoor shoots and the animations involved, it was Ray's most expensive film till then. *GGBB* became a run-away hit

---

[7]ibid., p.183.

making it his most commercially successful film and one of the biggest hits of Bengali cinema of all time in the box office.

GGBB had several songs, all written and composed by Ray himself. Ray had already started writing stories for his films by then and with this newfound confidence of being the lyricist and song composer, he delved into a sequel to *GGBB*, *Hirak Rajar Deshe*, in 1980. An allegorical satire, the film ran into certain political controversies. The script, with rhyming dialogues as short quips, is drawn heavily from Ray's father Sukumar Ray's literary works. Ray made this film in colour. Most importantly, though Goopy and Bagha remain the protagonists, there were a flock of child actors in *Hirak Rajar Deshe*. They are depicted in a group as the student class and not individually, but succeed in making the audience identify with them.

Two other Ray films which fall under the 'children's film' genre are both based on the detective character, Feluda. The first of these films, *Sonar Kella* (1974), was set in Rajasthan and revolved round Mukul, who is a young boy with the ability to remember events from a past life. Due to this special ability, Mukul is a child with an unusual gravitas in his personality. Kushal Chakraborty, who plays Mukul, remains one of the finest examples of child actors on the Indian screen. Robinson holds him in the same class actresses as Chandana Banerjee's Ratan in *Postmaster*. Ray, a reserved person himself, was unusually generous in his admiration for Kushal: 'He was exceedingly gifted. And he seemed quite unaware of the camera, completely stage-free and unselfconscious. A very rare kind of boy. I don't think I have come across any other boy so free from nervousness.'[8] For Kushal, the main reason why Ray is one of the better directors of child actors lies in his ability to instill confidence in the young minds that brings out the best in them:

He treated his child actors as adults. I remember after the editing for *Sonar Kella* was finished, he wanted to add a sequence which we didn't shoot before and which was probably not there in the script. He told me he wanted a scene where I cry, that would show the transformation to the final scene where I laugh. So he asked me whether I would be able to do that, if I could then he would build the sets at Indrapuri Studio at a cost of Rs 25,000 more. This kind of an attitude injects so much confidence in a child.[9]

---

[8]ibid., p.234.

[9]Kushal Chakraborty, 'Remembering Ray, Frame by Frame', *The Telegraph*, 02 May 2006, https://www.telegraphindia.com/1060502/asp/calcutta/story_6171959.asp, accessed on 15 May 2017

Kushal was also supposed to work in the next Feluda film *Joy Baba Felunath*, which was made after a gap of four years, but was eventually left out since he had grown a lot taller by then. Kushal grew up to become an engineer but unlike all other child actors in Ray films—except Soham (the child in *Shakha Proshakha* who is a commercial hero of mainstream Bengali cinema now)—he continued acting, and was reasonably popular for quite some time primarily in Television and occasionally in feature films. He continues acting in Television and doubles up as a director of serials and Television shorts.

The second Feluda film, *Joy Baba Felunath,* is different from its predecessor on many grounds. While *Sonar Kella* is as much an adventure film, thanks to the Rajasthan locale, as it is a detective one, *Joy Baba Felunath* is relatively static. Also, the basic crime being corruption, it is more sombre film than your usual children's film. In addition, unlike *Sonar Kella*, the primary focus is not on a child. The young grandson Ruku (played by a sprightly young boy Jit Bose) has a crucial importance in the final unfolding of the drama. Nonetheless, he is never as important as Mukul in *Sonar Kella*. Ray didn't make any other Feluda films after *Joy Baba Felunath,* to the dismay of his fans. Much later, Ray's son Sandip started adapting Feluda stories, first for Television and then for the big screen. Needless to say, the famous trio of Feluda, Jatayu and Topse had to be changed from Ray's favourties.

In the Feluda stories, Feluda's assistant is his cousin Topse, a teenager. Topse is someone who is in that twilight zone, waiting to embark into adulthood. For the two Ray films, the master had cast Siddhartha Chatterjee as Topse. Sandip Ray, who assisted Satyajit on these two, comments, 'Siddhartha was not in tune with the Feluda stories, so Baba gave him the script and he ended up doing a brilliant job.'[10] Like almost every actor who found a role in one of his films, Ray also observed Siddhartha silently at the time of their first meeting:

> Sometime later the bell rang. Siddhartha's father rose to answer the door. Ray stopped him. 'Why don't you see who it is, Siddhartha,' his voice was sonorous, but his tone sounded gentle. Siddhartha rose and walked to the door... Ray later said that he wanted to check out Siddhartha's

---

[10]Sandip Ray, 'Who Is the Best Topshe To Have Accompanied Feluda on Screen?', *Times Of India web edition,* 09 December 2014, http://timesofindia.indiatimes.com/entertainment/bengali/movies/Who-is-the-best-Topshe-to-have-accompanied-Felu-da-on-screen/Who-is-the-best-Topshe-to-have-accompanied-Felu-da-on-screen/photostory/45435160.cms, accessed on 15 May 2017.

ease in doing something as simple as opening a door in the rather uncomfortable setting of someone else's house. And Siddhartha himself has confirmed that when he found that the person who had come to meet Ray was Soumitra Chatterjee, a known face by then, he knew something major was happening. Later that year, they were off to Rajasthan for outdoor shooting.[11]

Siddhartha acted effortlessly in both the Feluda films. He remains the quintessential Topse, who is unobtrusively present besides Feluda's charismatic personality. A chartered accountant by profession, Siddhartha fondly remembers the shooting of *Joy Baba Felunath* in 1978:

There was a scene where Jatayu (Santosh Datta) and I had to dress like sadhus and wait at the ghat for Felu-da's instructions. So, we got off the car, a little before the ghat, with make-up and costumes. Some people at the ghat mistook us for real sadhus! And they took us to be pretty important sadhus probably because they had seen us getting off a car. Two local residents

---

[11]Mritika Sen, 'He Looked at Children through Their Eyes', *Deccan Herald*, 09 December 2005, http://archive.deccanherald.com/Deccanherald/dec92005/sesame164062005128.asp, accessed on 15 May 2017.

immediately bent down to touch Jatayu's feet and seek his blessings. Jatayu said, 'Tathastu!', and walked away. I turned to him, surprised. He said, 'Abhinoy korchhi jokhon continuous korte hobe. Majhkhane chharle hobe na (Since we are acting, we have to continue doing it. We can't quit midway)!' As there would be a huge crowd to watch the shooting, the film unit came up with a great plan. We would place a camera somewhere and spread the word that we were shooting in that area. Soon people would start thronging that spot, while we would be shooting elsewhere![12]

---

[12]'Siddhartha "Topshe" Chatterjee Relives His Joi Baba Felunath Days', *The Telegraph*, 15 February 2010, https://www.telegraphindia.com/1100215/jsp/entertainment/story_12105702.jsp, accessed on 15 May 2017.

THE SIGNIFICANT OTHERS

In his seminal work on Ray, *Satyajit Ray: The Inner Eye*, Andrew Robinson mentions, 'Ray has no taboo about the actors he selects. He has worked with every type of person, from box-office stars like Waheeda Rehman and Uttam Kumar, to people who had never seen a film, like the old relative of Sarbajaya in *Aparajito*.'[1] Robinson continues,

> Occasionally he selects someone from among the many people who come to his flat in the hope of getting a part, but usually—and especially in the earlier period of his career—he and his assistants and friends have to go out and get people, visiting all sorts of places on the off-chance of seeing the kind of face that Ray, with his skill as an illustrator, had pictured in his mind.[2]

This reading of Ray's handling of his cast is mostly accurate. Ray had utilized the services of both professional and non-professional actors, alongside turning quite a few non-professional actors into full-time ones after their debut in his films.

---

[1]Andrew Robinson, *Satyajit Ray: The Inner Eye*, Rupa and Co, 1990, p. 310.
[2]ibid.

MAGNIFICENT MEN

Pahari Sanyal was already a formidable actor who dabbled in both—the Bengali and Hindi film industries—when he first featured in a cameo role in Ray's *Paras Pathar*. The particular party scene, which is the climax of the film, has Pahari Sanyal almost playing himself as a film star. Sanyal, however, had a more important role in *Kanchenjungha* as the ornithologist uncle of the heroine. Routinely in many commercial Bengali films of that generation, Chhabi Biswas and Pahari Sanyal were like chalk-and-cheese, one dominant and haute and the other caring and sublime. Even within the ensemble cast, Sanyal gives a measured performance quite expressive to his theatrical prowess. Sanyal's last appearance in Ray's oeuvre was in another ensemble film, *Aranyer Din Ratri,* which is compared with *Kanchenjungha* by many critics due to their similar fervour. Again a poignantly subdued role, Pahari Sanyal played a retired service man and father of Aparna (played by Sharmila Tagore). The most notable point about Sanyal's contribution is the song, *Sey Daake Aamare* by Atul Prasad Sen, which he rendered in his own voice.

Kali Banerjee first appeared in a Ray film alongside Sanyal in *Paras Pathar* as the young secretary of Paresh Nath Dutta (Tulsi Chakraborty). Banerjee by then had already made his mark in the initial films by film-makers, who later became famous, such as Mrinal Sen's first film *Raat Bhore* (1955), Tapan Sinha's *Ankush* (1954), *Tonsil* (1956), *Kabuliwala* (1957) and Ritwik Ghatak's *Ajantrik* (1958). He was equally adept in typical mainstream films, including *Barjatri* (1951), *Nababidhan* (1954), *Sabar Upare* (1955), *Shilpi* (1956) and *Suryatoran* (1958), which made him an important star of the Bengali industry alongside the likes of Uttam Kumar, Bikas Roy, Basanta Chowdhury and later, Soumitra Chatterjee. In *Paras Pathar*, Kali Banerjee plays Priyatosh Henry Biswas, a young Bengali Christian. He has a girlfriend with whom he speaks secretly over the telephone. Banerjee provides a nuanced performance as a modern, urban, smart man who is fashionable and sleek. Yet, when faced with a crisis he crumbles and becomes a lovable Bengali boy who ultimately needs a lot of pampering. Banerjee next appears in *Monihara* (the second segment of the three-part *Teen Kanya*) as Phanibhusan, a wealthy man with a psychotic wife who is obsessed with gems, jewels and gaudy ornaments. Phanibhusan's character is the complete opposite of Priyatosh due to the difference in time, social and financial positions, and the love-relations the two characters deal with. While Priyatosh is still falling in love with his girlfriend he is yet to marry, for Phanibhusan, the ghost of his wife, who drowned, keeps coming back again and again to haunt him.

Alongside Kali Banerjee, another impressive character actor of Bengali cinema who didn't get his due recognition is Jnanesh Mukherjee. Mukherjee acted in Ritwik Ghatak's *Meghe Dhaka Tara* and *Jukti Tokko Goppo*, Mrinal Sen's *Baishe Sraban*, *Akash Kusum* and *Mrigaya*, Rajen Tarafdar's *Ganga* apart from Ray's *Abhijan*. Incidentally, like Kali in *Paras Pathar*, Jnanesh plays a Christian character (named Joseph) in *Abhijan*.

Arun Mukherjee was part of the legendary Sambhu Mitra's theatre group, Bohurupee. The story goes that Ray spotted him in one of their theatre productions and decided to cast him as Ashok in *Kanchenjungha,* a role which Soumitra Chatterjee wanted to play but couldn't due to date issues. Mukherjee went on to make quite a few films after *Kanchenjungha,* including *Mansoor Miyanar Ghora,* but the former was his only one with Ray. Rumour has it that Ray contemplated casting Arun in *Goopy Gyne Bagha Byne* as well, but somehow that never happened.

Three other Bengali actors who have acted in Ray's cinema and need to be mentioned are Dipankar Dey, Subhendu Chatterjee and Victor Banerjee. However, it is difficult to categorize them into individual profiles with strong and unique traits like the other profiles in this book. Dey first acted in a small cameo in *Seemabaddha* in 1971, followed by a slightly bigger one five years later in *Jana Aranya*. However, his main association with Ray happened during the master's last three films—*Ganashatru, Shakha Prashakha* and *Agantuk*. Though not villainous in the classical sense of the term, Dey's roles in all the three films have distinct shades of black—enough to make them quite despicable, if not hated. Dey gave a measured performance in all of them. Recollecting his experience with Ray, Dipankar insisted that he found Satyajit very easy to work with:

> ...this man doesn't impose his ideas on actors, he gives his actors a free hand except in the roles where some nuances, and innuendos need to be shown. He used to act those scenes to demonstrate what he wants from the actor... In fact, the way he used to read his scripts and portray different characters to the artists, I don't think any of us could give even 75% of his performances.[3]

In *Ganashatru*, Subhendu plays Biresh, who is an assistant editor to Haridas (Dipankar Dey) at a daily newspaper. However, Subhendu first appeared in Ray's *Chiriyakhana* in 1967 as Ajit, the assistant to the mercurial sleuth

---

[3]Dipankar Dey Interview, 'Why Satyajit Ray Wanted To Slap Dipankar De', *News18.com*, 02 May 2012, http://www.news18.com/news/india/why-satyajit-ray-wanted-to-slap-dipankar-de-470593.html, accessed on 15 May 2017.

Byomkesh Bakshi played by Uttam Kumar. Subhendu debuted two years previously in Mrinal Sen's classic *Akash Kusum,* where he played second fiddle to Soumitra Chatterjee. Though he went on to become one of the bankable heroes of Bengali cinema (similar to Dipankar Dey and Victor Banerjee), he remained perpetually in the shadows of both Uttam Kumar and Soumitra Chatterjee in terms of popularity and definite acting calibre. The second performance of Subhendu in a Ray film was in the masterpiece *Aranyer Din Ratri* where he got the chance to play Sanjay—perhaps his biggest and most important role in Ray's cinema. Reminiscing about the acting experience in the film, Subhendu remarked:

> The country liquor shop which was shown in the film was an original one. Most of the people who were there in the shop were local people unaware that they were being filmed... Before the start of shooting, Manik-da would call everyone involved for a script-reading session. He would act it out so well that unless you have been there you won't believe the acting prowess he had. Even before a shot was being taken he used to show how to act the scene out—it was so excellent that if you can reproduce even fifty percent of that you will be considered as a great actor. Even Uttam Kumar

told me that he could imitate only fifty percent of what Manik-da showed in *Nayak* and seventy percent in *Chiriyakhana*. Uttam Kumar got the best actor award for *Chiriyakhana*! ...he(Ray) would give liberty to actors if he could sense that the actor has a natural gift. Otherwise he would give minute details as to how to turn the head, when to frown and so on.[4]

Victor Banerjee had a completely different trajectory though—something which no other Bengali actor can boast about. In 1984, Banerjee enacted the role of Dr Aziz Ahmed in David Lean's *A Passage to India,* which instantly made him an international star and for which he was nominated for the prestigious BAFTA award. However, Banerjee appeared earlier in Ray's maiden Hindi feature film *Shatranj Ke Khilari* as the prime minister. Banerjee recounts his association with Ray and how he got his role in the movie:

Utpal Dutt was originally meant to launch me into films; until I happened to walk away. He made an appointment for me to meet Satyajit Ray. He was impressed with my file of reviews, which

[4]Subhendu Chatterjee Interview, 'Satyajit Ray and Aranyer Din Ratri Special Issue', *Chitravas*, Vol 40 (No. 1 to 4), January–December 2005, p. 103.

included praise lavished on me by critics like the noted sceptic Dharani Ghosh of Calcutta, and the staid and reticent Khalid Mohammed in Bombay. That, coupled with the fact that I lied through my teeth when asked if I spoke Urdu, did the trick [of getting the role of the prime minister in *Shatranj Ke Khilari*]. Manik-da genuinely liked what I was doing. Mind you, I was the lone Bengali in his principal cast of Bombay actors. When the final rushes arrived, he took producer Suresh Jindal along with other connoisseurs of Bombay like Javed Siddiqui and Shama Zaidi to watch my scene standing by a door, staring at the crestfallen Nawab of Awadh. Manik-da did more publicity for me than anyone else. It was the beginning of an association of mutual admiration, where both brooked criticism and gloated praise.[5]

Banerjee continued to make his mark in the films of reputed directors, including James Ivory (*Hullabaloo over Georgie and Bonnie's Pictures*) and Shyam Benegal (*Kalyug, Arohan*) before working in Ray's favourite project—the adaptation of Rabindranath Tagore's *Ghare Baire*. *Ghare*

---

[5]Victor Banerjee, 'It Was the Beginning of an Association of Mutual Admiration', *Forbes India*, 12 May 2015, http://www.forbesindia.com/printcontent/40187, accessed on 15 May 2017.

Baire remained Victor's last film with Ray, for which he won the Best Supporting Actor award at the 32nd National Film Awards. Banrejee's Nikhilesh against Soumitra Chatterjee's marvelous villain-incarnate Sandip is an even match with Bimala (Swatilekha Chatterjee) as the fulcrum. Victor Banerjee also worked in a short film, *Pikoo*, by Ray in 1981 before *Ghare Baire*. The film, commissioned for a French Television channel, was complex, where Banerjee played the role of an illicit lover of a married woman.

Shatranj Ke Khilari was important for being Ray's only Hindi feature film. Due to this, it was primarily a film where Ray had to depend on professional actors of the Hindi film industry. Ray roped in mainstream stars including Sanjeev Kumar and Amjad Khan (of Gabbar Singh fame) alongside versatile actors, viz. Saeed Jaffrey and Tom Alter, apart from the legendary actor/filmmaker Sir Richard Attenborough, who played the role of Lord Outram. Saeed Jaffrey, who was a big admirer of Ray, had wanted to act in his films since he had watched *Pather Panchali* in Delhi before crossing over to Great Britain. Jaffrey was the most prominent face among the Asian and Indian actors in Britain during the '70s and '80s before becoming a known face in Hindi cinema as well. His foray into Hindi films was inaugurated by his extremely nuanced portrayal of Mir

Roshan Ali in *Shatranj Ke Khilari,* for which he won the Filmfare Best Supporting Actor Award. Recalling his association with Ray, Jaffrey said,

> He's a man of such wide sympathies, such a gentle, shy person on so many levels—artist, musician, scholar and all the rest—that it's almost frightening. He is very much a man of nuances. His precision in what he wants from his actors is so acute, his emphasis on detail so all-encompassing that it becomes challenging and easy work at the same time. For me it was a period of heightened excitement.[6]

ELOQUENT ACTRESSES

In the early part of the '70s, a new wave lapped the shores of Hindi cinema. Spearheaded by the likes of Shyam Benegal, Govind Nihalanai and others, this 'new wave' also marked the advent of a class of rare actors who defied the prevalent star system in lieu of a natural, realistic style of acting. At the forefront were four actors who, till date, remain India's finest film actors

---

[6]'Saeed Jaffrey: Long Way from Home', *India Today*, 1 April 2014, http://indiatoday.intoday.in/story/saeed-jaffrey-long-way-from-home/1/428022.html, accessed on 02 April 2017.

of all time—Naseeruddin Shah, Om Puri, Shabana
Azmi and Smita Patil. Satyajit Ray's cinema rarely had
characters which this quartet could enact and as a result,
Naseeruddin never worked with Ray. Shabana starred
in a minor yet significant role in *Shatranj Ke Khilari* as the
wife of Mirza Sajjad Ali (Sanjeev Kumar). However,
in Ray's heart-wrenching short film *Sadgati*, both Om
Puri and Smita Patil, along with Mohan Agashe, showed
their acting abilities to the fullest and justified their
prowess. For Smita Patil's short, yet extremely eventful
and remarkable career, *Sadgati* remains an important
film. As veteran film critic Chidananda Dasgupta
mentioned,

> It is hard to think of a better embodiment of
> the poor rural slum woman than Smita. In the
> fineries of the upper class, she always seemed a
> misfit as in *Arth* and in the commercials she did
> towards the end of her unduly short career. At
> most she shone as the middle or lower middle class
> woman of *Ardhsatya* or *Subah*. But as the milkmaid
> of *Manthan*, the slum dweller of *Chakra* or the chilli
> sorter of *Mirch Masala* she really belonged.[7]

Much before Smita Patil acted in a Ray film, two other

---

[7]Chidananda Dasgupta, *The Cinema of Satyajit Ray*, National Book Trust,
India, 2003, p. 124.

Bollywood actresses, with different acting capacities and box-office followings, acted in Ray's films. When Waheeda Rehman acted in *Abhijan*—incidentally one of Ray's most commercially successful films—it was indeed big news, mostly because such a big star of Hindi cinema had never before acted in a Bengali film. Rehman played Gulaabi, the prostitute-turned-mistress of a corrupt Marwari businessman who is eventually rescued by the Rajput taxi driver Narsingh played by Soumitra Chatterjee. In her memoir, Rehman recollected how she got associated with *Abhijan:*

> The editor of *Filmfare*, B.K. Karanjia, sent someone to my house with a letter from Mr Ray that said: 'My leading man Soumitra Chatterjee and my unit believe that you are most suitable for the role of Gulaabi, the heroine of my next film. If you agree to play the part, we'll be very pleased.' I was very happy and could not believe Satyajit Ray had thought of me... A few days later I called Mr Ray in Calcutta and the first thing he said was: 'Waheeda, you earn a lot of money in Hindi films. I make films on small budgets.' 'Saab, why are you embarrassing me? It is an honour for me. You have shown me much respect by asking me to work with you. There is no problem about the

money. I prefer you don't mention it.' I explained to him that I didn't speak Bengali, and he said the character he wanted me to play, Gulaabi, is from the Bihar-Bengal border and talks in a mix of Bhojpuri and Bengali. Therefore, the language should not be a problem for me.[8]

Waheeda was awestruck with Ray's meticulous detailing and working style:

He sketched every scene and made detailed shot breakdowns, even noting the lens he planned to use. His storyboarding was extremely helpful. In those days no one had heard of storyboarding. He was also one of the few directors who gave me a bound script. There was a scene in *Abhijan* where I am sitting in a *ghoda gaadi* (horse carriage) and a *sethji* is forcibly taking me away. Soumitra (Chatterjee) comes, I look at him and jump out of the carriage and run away. Before Ray Saab could say anything to me, I glanced at the *sethji* and jumped out. Mr Ray quickly said: 'I was about to ask you to do just that. But you did it before I could say anything!'...
Satyajit Ray made films the way films should be

---

[8]'Conversations with Waheeda Rehman', *Live Mint*, 29 March 2014, http://www.livemint.com/Leisure/fGObeCYbUyGXq8fmV5c3VK/Excerpt--Conversations-With-Waheeda-Rehman.html, accessed on 15 May 2017.

made—from start to finish. So whether you're
needed on the set or not, you can spend your
whole time thinking about your character. It's not
just about learning the dialogue and facing the
camera, you must somewhat live the role and not
always be acting it.[9]

When Satyajit Ray announced the casting of *Aranyer Din
Ratri,* it had a few sparks. Firstly, it was an ensemble
cast much like *Kanchenjungha,* which, somehow had
not been greatly received by the critics or the public.
Secondly, it was a comeback film for Kaberi Bose who
was a rising star in the '50s, often paired with Uttam
Kumar, and who had left the film industry in pursuit
of a family life. It was reported that Bose had publicly
remarked that she would contemplate returning to
the silver screen only if Satyajit Ray asked her to play
a role in his film. Bose eventually delivered a very
uniquely passionate performance as a young widow who
is reserved yet not shy to portray her inner feelings.
The third and biggest surprise was the casting of Simi
Garewal in the role of a tribal girl. For Simi, the offer
was almost like a pleasant shock:

How could anyone envision that a 'westernized and

---

[9]ibid.

sophisticated' girl like me could play an Adivasi tribal woman? But then, I guess that's what sets a great director apart... We journeyed to Chhipadohar by train and car. For a week Manik-da wouldn't let me shoot. He'd take me to the 'baati-khaana' (the liquor shop) where the Adivasis would gather at night to drink—and let me just observe. I saw women who were exactly like 'Duli', my character, and it made it all so easy. I relished my transformation. It took four hours to cover me with the black paint (even in my ears!)—and it took 3 hours to remove it later! And in the in-between I became another being, rustic, uninhibited, untutored and raw. Manik-da would come to our cottage after pack-up to play word games. But first he would show me the story-board sketches of the next day's shoot— and I would know exactly how he had conceived the scene frame-by-frame. It was then that I became fascinated with direction. I make similar story boards when I direct now, following his line of homework. It was a turning point in my life.[10]

Rumour has it that Lily Chakraborty was called by Ray while he was scouting for Aparna for *Apur Sansar*.

---

[10]'Aranyer Din Ratri', *Simi Garewal website*, http://www.simigarewal.com/aranyer_din_ratri.html, accessed on 15 May 2017.

Photographs of Lily were taken after dressing her up as Aparna (something Ray did with many actors new to his cinema—specially the actresses, including Sharmila Tagore and Aparna Sen).

> Manik-da told me that he had liked me very much but there was another girl he had already selected, though her parents were hesitant. 'If they agree to let their daughter act in my film then I won't be able to take you,' Manik-da told me. Later, we came to know that Sharmila Tagore got the role.[11]

Lily, however, got to act in a couple of Ray films—*Jana Aranya* and *Shakha Prashakha*—and in both she played a loving and lovable sister-in-law who conforms to the norms of a Hindu patriarchal society and strives hard to uphold them.

As an extension of the homely bride of the family, we find Ananga in *Ashani Sanket* for which Ray cast Babita, a popular Bangladeshi actress. Babita's charming innocent face and the lilt in her expression conveyed the necessary reactions. For Babita, like most of the actors new to Ray's cinema, the working experience was altogether different—something she never experienced in Bangladesh:

---

[11]'Was Surprised to Receive a Letter from Manik-da All of a Sudden', Interview of Lily Chakraborty, *Saptahik Bartaman*, 11 April 1992, p. 22.

In his script, on every page on the left, he would draw how we would shoot the individual shots—whether it will be a close-up or a mid-shot or an over-the-shoulder shot. And on the right the corresponding dialogues were there. It was a very unique experience for me. In Dhaka most of our outdoor shootings used to happen in broad daylight. In *Ashani Sanket* I found that Manik-da was shooting mostly in part-cloudy atmosphere... Maybe he thought that I resembled Ananga bou to quite an extent. Mostly, he never told me anything about how to enact the character. Only a few times he would say very politely that he would take the shot again. I would understand then that probably he wasn't pleased with the shot and hence wanted a retake.[12]

Quite opposite to this domesticated profile, the docile wife gives way to Bimala—Tagore's independent heroine in the famous *Ghare Baire*. The film was shelved multiple times and got indefinitely postponed for various reasons including the fact that Ray was not happy with the actresses he auditioned for portraying the role of Bimala. Finally, Ray zeroed in on Swatilekha Chatterjee who had

[12]*Actress Babita on Director Satyajit Ray and Zahir Raihan*, https://www.youtube.com/watch?v=owPpLE2cbdQ, accessed on 15 May 2017.

never acted in films but had a theatre background in Nandikar, a leading theatre group of Bengal. Ray did admit that he had initial doubts, considering Swatilekha was from Allahabad and had an English-medium schooling background. Ray had watched Swatilekha in the Bengali versions of two foreign plays—*Schweyk in the Second World War* and *Galileo Galilei*—and noticed her personality and intelligence. However, when Ray met Swatilekha, his doubts about her fitting the role of a modern Bengali woman from the late nineteenth or early twentieth century were allayed:

> I had a kind of faith in Swatilekha, and I was tempted to have her for Bimala. Then I finally found that her Bengali is also fluent, she has confidence, intelligence, she wouldn't have any difficulty understanding the character...she was capable of comprehending the character— she has the intellect to 'understand' what she was doing, not just instinctively, but acting with intelligence...after the first day's work, I came to have full confidence in her.[13]

Swatilekha Chatterjee as Bimala, however, did not match up to the expectations of the Tagore puritans and

---

[13]Jayanti Sen, 'From Pather Panchali to Ghare Bairey: An Interview with Satyajit Ray', *Cinewave* Vol 5, January–March 1984, p. 9.

the common viewers alike. The brightness of Bimala—
not only her physical beauty but also her acumen—
were perhaps missing. Especially after the brilliant
Madhabi Mukherjee in *Charulata,* the expectations of a
fitting Bimala in Ray's *Ghare Baire* were paramount. The
uninitiated audience didn't understand why two most
eligible, smart and handsome men—Nikhilesh (Victor
Banerjee) and Sandeep (Soumitra Chatterjee)—would
be enamoured by the captive brilliance of Bimala. The
film's structure, however, had many of the classical
touches of Ray's cinematic aesthetics. For Swatilekha the
experience was worthwhile—

> Ray doesn't discuss the scene, character or
> implications of interaction at great length. The
> guidance he gives is brief and suggestive... With
> him, the actor has the freedom to interpret his
> role but always it is Ray who has the last word...
> Does Ray have different ways of guiding different
> actors? Perhaps yes. I saw that he directed Victor
> Banerjee more than the veteran Ray-hero Soumitra
> Chatterjee. Ray has every scene planned and
> thought-processed, right down to the whispers
> and silences. So the improvisations at shooting are
> based on a fully worked-out master plan.[14]

---

[14]Swatilekha Sengupta (Chatterjee) interview, 'The Genius of Satyajit Ray

In his last three films, when Ray's journey was more inwards, the one constant factor was the presence of Mamata Shankar (along with Dipankar Dey) in the cast. Mamata Shankar in *Ganashatru* and *Agantuk* brought in a new character profile hitherto unknown and undiscovered in Ray's oeuvre. It was that of the daughter. In *Pather Panchali*, Ray's first, the daughter Durga died prematurely, closing this profile. The young women in Ray's cinema more often than not played the heroine, like Aparna (Sharmila Tagore in *Apur Sansar* and *Aranyer Din Ratri*), Mrinmoyee (Aparna Sen in *Samapti*) and others. As the central character in Ray's cinema aged with him, it was probably imperative that the next generation should find their legitimate place in the script. Since the late '70s, Ray had actually taken up stories where the family was not at the fore (the Feluda films or *Hirak Rajar Deshe*) or, as in *Ghare Baire*, it was the sexual tension between three individuals in the backdrop of the Indian freedom movement that held sway. Perhaps, there was no better young Bengali actress at that time than Mamata Shankar to feature in the profile of a 'daughter'. Shankar was a brilliant actress already, being a constant face in the films of Mrinal Sen, Goutam Ghose and Buddhadeb Dasgupta.

Issue', *Frontline* magazine, 20 December 1991, p. 89.

So, when Ray called her up for *Ganashatru,* it was a dream come true for her:

Have you ever read a huge book with innumerable pages, bringing new surprises every turn? Well, to me Manik-kaka is like that. The more I observe him the more dazed I get. At first, believing him to be always aloof and serious, I quailed in his presence. But with my first film under his direction I realised that he was kind, approachable and considerate. Never have I seen him accept a cup of tea without making sure that the whole unit had its share. A director of his stature might well overlook such details, but these little gestures of his touched me deeply. You know how painstakingly careful he is of every aspect of his craft—sets, lighting, costumes and so on. But he is equally particular that every artist should feel comfortable with these arrangements. He never starts shooting until he checks out with them. During the shooting of *Ganashatru* I suffered from acute backache. Manik-kaka had me always provided with a chair in between shots. This kind of individual attention amidst the myriad problems of film-making is certainly rare. You can see that he had genuine respect for others. During the shooting of *Agantuk* when I requested him to let me do a scene again, he agreed at once, though finally he retained the earlier shot. But he was thoughtful about assuaging my anxiety over the performance. Familiarity increases one's admiration for Manik-kaka's personality. All of us who work for him feel privileged to have the opportunities for close interaction with a man of his knowledge and experience. No one would dare take liberties with him, but each one feels engulfed by his warmth and concern.[15]

Before entering into Ray's house of cinema, Shankar had acted in four films by Mrinal Sen, *Mrigayaa*, *Oka Oori Katha*, *Ek Din Pratidin* and *Kharij*, where the characters were diverse—from an unmarried tribal woman to a middle-class Bengali mother. She, like many who have acted in both Ray and Sen's films, found the essential difference between the two stalwarts:

They were entirely different. Mrinal-da was very spontaneous like he might have the script and then he might have gone to the location, and then something might inspire him to construct a scene

[15]Mamata Shankar Interview, 'The Genius of Satyajit Ray Issue', *Frontline* magazine, 20 December 1991, p. 89.

then and there. He was normally very relaxed with the script. On the other hand Manik-kaka had everything planned, everything chalked out. He had a red note book 'kherol khata' in which every shot was sketched...he never forced anything on us. Firstly, he would read out the script and he wanted all his actors to be present during the narration session. He would suggest changes but while shooting he just watched the performances on the screen, and if he felt that certain things need to be done then only he would interfere otherwise he would leave everything to the actors... He was disciplined but not strict in that sense. He had his own style, I never saw him getting angry. He would never criticise anyone publicly. Even if he wanted to take another shot, he would say we have to take another shot due to some technical failure, and since we are doing this again can we improvise a little.[16]

Most of the actors and actresses, seasoned or amateur, have all revered Ray's handling of his cast, which allowed them a lot of liberties but guided them when

---

[16]'Never Saw Satyajit Ray Angry: Mamata Shankar', *News18.com*, http://www.news18.com/news/india/never-saw-satyajit-ray-angry-mamata-shankar-470569.html, 2 May 2012, accessed on 15 May 2017.

needed as well. It is indeed important to note that apart from a handful of miscast cases, Ray was deft in finding the appropriate actor or actress for his different roles, including cameos. Alakananda Roy who played Manisha, the shy, timid yet independent younger daughter of a wealthy aristocrat in *Kanchenjungha,* summed up what Ray meant to his cast:

> Manik-da used to talk to me about the role for hours. This made the entire thing very easy for me. Every day before the shot he would explain the situation to me and would say, 'Are you able to understand Manisha's thoughts in this?' he would discuss with me till I was absolutely certain. Then he would provide me with the dialogue. We never memorized any of the dialogues. I didn't have much problem in getting the essence of the character. Actually Manisha and I were of the same age group and both of us were from Presidency College. Maybe Manik-da chose me for the role because of this background.[17]

Alakananda provided an anecdote which brings to light another aspect of Ray—his ability to make changes to his script at the last moment—a trait which most of his cast

---

[17]'Had a Beggar Boy Sing a Song in Kanchenjungha', Interview of Alakananda Roy, *Saptahik Bartaman*, 11 April 1992, p. 18.

tended to overlook under the guise of Ray's disciplinary methods:

> Manik-da wrote the script in Darjeeling. When he went there at that time he found a small beggar boy who had a very melodious voice. Later, when we all came for the shooting he asked his unit to find the boy. Manik-da soon became friends with him and eventually added him in his script. The boy became famous by being in *Kanchenjungha*. At the end of the film we can find him eating chocolates and singing a very melodious tune.[18]

---

[18]ibid.

ACKNOWLEDGEMENTS

This book belongs to all lovers of Satyajit Ray's cinema. In the summer of 2016 when I started writing this book, little did I know that it would grow on me like a huge canvas and haunt me for days and months for over a year. It gave me the opportunity to go back and watch all the Ray films once again, systematically, together and one after the other in the form of a retrospective. With all great works of art, every reading brings new perspectives, diverse meanings and fresh reflections on life and culture.

I am particularly indebted to Mr Shiladitya Sarkar, painter, writer and a dear friend, for some of the best conversations on Ray which definitely helped me to structure the book and devise its trajectory. I am also indebted to Father Gaston Roberge. We seldom discussed this book, but in the past, we did talk on cinema and of Ray in our multiple meetings in his quaint chamber in St Xaviers College, Kolkata. I am sure those discussions hold their meaning in my interpretation of Ray's profiles. I am also indebted to veteran film scholar Dr Shoma A. Chatterji for her relentless inspiration— both by being herself and her phenomenal energy of writing—and by her direct prodding and pushing me to come out of my languor and complete this book.

Any writing on the cinema of Ray is incomplete without major references to Soumitra Chatterjee—an actor who featured in fourteen Ray films and who is almost like Ray's alter-ego on celluloid. I was fortunate enough to write a book on him—*Beyond Apu—20 Favourite Film Roles of Soumitra Chatterjee*—published in 2016. Soumitra Babu (as I refer to him) gave me several insights into Ray's cinema, not only during that book but even after while I was writing this one. His generosity is paramount. I am grateful to Sharmila Tagore and Madhabi Mukherjee for endorsing the book. My heartfelt thanks is extended to my friend Mimi Bhattacharya, daughter of Madhabi Mukherjee, for her generous support and help.

I am also deeply indebted to professor Moinak Biswas, film-maker and professor of Film Studies, Jadavpur University, Ms Subha Das Mollick, film-maker, critic and teacher, and Ms Sumita Samanta, scholar and publisher, for their valuable inputs regarding the different aspects of this book.

Mr Pinaki De who has kindly agreed to design the cover of this book is a friend and well-wisher. Pinaki obliged me earlier by designing the cover of my previous book as well. I cannot express enough, my gratitude towards him. I am grateful to Asit Poddar, photographer, painter and one who has observed Ray up close, not only for the photographs he shared with me for this book, but also for the insight on the legend. I am deeply obliged to Sandip Ray, film-maker and Ray's son, and also The Society for the Preservation of Satyajit

Ray Archives for providing me with stills of his films.

At home, my family supported me through thick and thin, without which I couldn't have completed the book. My ten-year-old son, Akash, who had watched a handful of Ray's films with me including *Apur Sansar* apart from the 'children's films', startled me with riveting questions which only a child can think of and ask. His inquisitions made me look at those films from a different perspective—a learning experience for me.

Satyajit Ray was a master illustrator and a very popular writer alongside his cinematic credence. The details of his characterizations in his drawings and in writings are stupendous. Within the ambit of his cinema as well, his genius is in creating so many characters who seem so real and lively. The characters are not only the heroes and heroines, but extend to the mundane shop-keeper, the edgy old men of the village, the sly public relations officer and many more. These make his cinema so fulfilling and so very identifiable. This book intends to embrace this diversity of Ray's cinema and document his extremely talented actors and actresses who brightened the screen— from one-off appearances to the regulars of his cinema.

I hope this book will make the reader go back to his films to appreciate the nuances of the master film-maker and the rich repertoire of excellent acting standards in his cinema.